Persian (Farsi-Dari)

Grammar and Self-Learner

Yavar Dehghani

Preface	5
Introduction to Persian	7
Introduction to grammar	9
Introduction to transliteration	12
Persian sound system	13
Persian alphabet	17
Guide for learning the lessons	19
Lesson 1: Greetings	20
Lesson 2: Introduction	22
Lesson 3: Languages	25
Lesson 4: Feelings	28
Lesson 5: Personal details	30
Lesson 6: Occupations	34
Lesson 7: Family	37
Lesson 8: Travel	42
Lesson 9: Weather	46
Lesson 10: At the restaurant	49
Lesson 11: Booking hotel	54
Lesson 12: Time and date	57
Lesson 13: Daily routines	60
Lesson 14: At the bank	64
Lesson 15: At the chemist	67
Lesson 16: At doctor's surgery	70

Lesson 17: At the supermarket   73

Lesson 18: Seasons   77

Lesson 19: In the park   80

Lesson 20: New Year   83

Grammar Section   86

Adjective   87

Adverb   87

Affix   87

Article   88

Auxiliary verbs   89

Causative verb   90

Classifiers   93

Colloquial forms   92

Comparative adjectives   93

Complementiser   94

Compound verbs   96

Conjunctions   97

Copula (tobe)   106

Difficult English words for Persian speakers 108

Double negative   109

English words with no equivalent in Persian 110

English words with different Persian meaning 110

Future tense   111

Greetings in Persian	113
Idioms	114
Imperatives	116
Infinitive	117
Intransitive verbs	118
Interrogatives (Questions)	120
Keš verb	123
Verbs plus prepositions	123
Negatives	125
Noun	127
Numbers	122
Object	128
Object marker rä	131
Passive voice	132
Past tense	133
Persian words with similar pronunciation	136
Persian words with different meanings	142
Person and number	143
Politeness	144
Possession	146
Prefix be-	149
Preposition	152
Present perfect tense	152
Present tense	153

Second verb	156
Pronoun	156
Sentence types	157
Subject	159
Suffixes	159
tä	160
Suffix –i (able)	161
Tag questions	161
tavän, xäh and dän	162
There & It	162
Transitive verbs	163
Verb	165
Verbs plus prepositions	166
Vowel *y*	166
Vowel *e*	166
Word če	167

Preface

This book is one of the most comprehensive books, which have been written in English to teach Persian (Farsi & Dari) as a second or foreign language. The uniqueness of this book is that:

a) It uses a comparative linguistics method to teach Persian as a second or foreign language. This method has been attested by the author through several years of teaching of Persian to adult English speakers in Australia. The logic behind this method is that if the language learners understand the structural differences between their own language and the target language, learning the language will be much easier for them.

b) It uses transliteration as the basis for teaching Persian, without using Arabic script, a non Roman alphabet. Therefore, the learners do not need to learn the script to be able to learn the language. That is, knowing the script is not a prerequisite for learning Persian, and so the learners can learn speaking in the language without reading and writing it.

Not being able to read the script has always been a problem for most English speakers who wanted to learn Persian. This problem has forced many of them to give up learning the language alltogether. The usefulness of transliteration has already been proved in the author's bidirectional English-Persian dictionary where the transliteration rather than the script is used for word entries.

c) Although many courses are offered for learning Persian around the world, there are few practical grammar book and self learners to use, and thus this book will hopefully fill the gap.

d) The practical grammatical subtleties and exceptions in the language are usually left out in textbooks. This leads the learners to fall into the traps of literal translation. In this book, these subtleties and exceptions are covered in the grammar section.

e) The current self-learner books always focus on Farsi variation of Persian and ignore the Dari variation. This makes them less useful for many learners who want to learn Dari to be able to communicate in Afghanistan. However, this book gives the alternatives in Dari on the footnotes, and thus the learner will be able to communicate in both Farsi of Iran and Dari of Afghanistan.

Introduction to Persian

Persian is a language of the Indo-Iranian family group which itself is a member of Indo-European languages. Indo-Iranian languages split into Iranian languages and Indic languages around 1500 BC. The major Iranian languages are Persian, Pashto, Kurdish, Gilaki and Baluchi. The main dialect of Persian is Farsi, which is spoken in Iran and is the official language of the country. The other dialects are Dari, which is spoken in Afghanistan, and Tajiki, which is spoken in Tajikistan[1]. These dialects are mutually intelligible. That is, the speakers of these dialects can communicate with each other very well. Most of the differences are with vocabulary. There are differences in pronunciation too. However, the difference in grammar is very little. In this book, the differences in vocabulary have been addressed as they are more important in communication in either dialect. However, as a general rule, if you learn one dialect, you will be able to communicate with the speakers of the other dialects. There are many Persian speakers in the neighbouring countries as well as in Europe and USA.

---

[1] There are debates about whether these three languages (Farsi, Dari and Tajiki) are three dialects of the same language, that is Persian, or they are separate languages. As the speakers of all these three languages understand each other effectively, they are considered as dialects in this book.

Old Persian was spoken from the beginning of the Achemenides Empire (around 550 BBC) until the conquest of Persia by Alexander the Great (around 330 BC) and was inscribed in Cuneiform. Middle Persian was spoken from 330 BC until the fall of Sassanid dynasty (around 7th century) when Arabs occupied Persian Empire. After the introduction of Islam in the Persian Empire, Arabic became the official language of Iran. Consequently, Persian language and literature was suppressed for almost two centuries. Modern Persian was emerged after this time, and the Arabic script was adopted for writing Persian. Since Arabic was the language of intellectuals, writers and poets as well as the administrators at the time, the modern Persian was heavily influenced by this language. That is why; there are a huge number of words in current Persian which are borrowed form Arabic.

Introduction to grammar

Grammar is very important in learning a second language. In a sense, grammar is a collection of rules that form words and sentences in a language. Therefore, we need to learn the grammar of that language to know how to speak the language, how to pronounce its sounds, how to make sentences, and so on.

Of course, as native speakers of our first language, we do not need to know its grammar, because as most linguists and psycholinguists agree, our brain in childhood is equipped with a language-learning device, which enables us to learn our mother tongue easily and without any special effort.

However, to learn another language as an adult, we need to know its grammar; otherwise we would need a lot of time and effort to learn the expressions in the language one by one, and it would be very time consuming.

The proverb: "If you give me a fish, you provide me a meal, but if you teach me how to fish, you give me my food for whole my life" is true for learning a second language. That is, if you teach a sentence in your language to others, they would know just one sentence in the language, but if you teach them how to make sentences in the language, they would know how to speak your language.

My experience in teaching a second language to students in different age groups has taught me that teaching grammar is the key to success in second language learning.

As mentioned before, since we do not need grammar for our own language as native speakers, most of us do not know the grammar and grammatical concepts of our languages. However, to learn a second language, and in this case Persian, we need to learn them.

Those students, who have difficulty in learning the grammar of a second language, have usually problems with the grammar of their own language too. Thus, by learning their own grammar, they would find it easier to learn another language. My experience with Persian or English students has shown that most students are reluctant to admit that they know nothing about their own language (grammar), and need to learn it. However, when they start to learn it, they appreciate how quickly they can learn the second language. That is why, in every course on Persian, I start with teaching English grammar, and when the students are familiar with the basic grammar of their own language, I teach Persian grammar.

In this book, you will get familiar with grammatical concepts throughout the lessons. Each grammar concept will be introduced within English context first and then it will be discussed in Persian. Comparing each grammatical concept in both languages will help you to learn Persian, as quickly and easily as possible.

Introduction to transliteration

Transliteration is a writing system with which the sounds of a language are written. The symbols in this system are the same for all languages. The purpose of this system is to enable the learners to read words and sentences in any language without learning their script. The symbols used in this system are similar to English with some minor differences. It especially makes the learning of languages with non Roman scripts like Arabic, Persian, Japanese, Korean, Khmer, Chinese, etc. easier for the learners of those languages. That is why; this system is used to teach the language to the Persian learners in this book.

Ordinarily, Persian self learner books use Persian script to teach the language to non native speakers. However, since learning the script especially before learning the sound system is hard and time consuming, most of beginners quit learning it altogether.

Persian sound system

In this book, there is no need to learn the script. You need the script only for reading and writing and not for speaking and listening! There are 29 transliteration symbols for Persian sounds: 6 for vowels and 23 for consonants:

Vowels: The vowel system in Persian is simple and just consists of six vowels. These vowels are:

a	as the 'a' in 'ask' and 'fast'
e	as the 'e' in 'get' and 'fell'
i	as the 'i' in 'fit' and 'pitch'
o	as the 'a' in 'ball' or the 'o' in 'mole'
u	as the 'u' in 'rule' and 'push'
ä	as the 'o' in 'top' or 'a' in 'father'

There are differences between short and long vowels for each of these. However, since they do not make a difference in meaning, they are not discussed for the sake of simplicity.

There are also subtle differences between vowels in Dari and Farsi. Again, since they do not make a difference in meaning, they are discussed in here.

Consonants: Most Persian consonants are pronounced like their English counterparts. The consonants, which are pronounced similar to the English ones, are listed here:

b	as the 'b' in 'boy'
č	as the 'ch' in 'cheese'
d	as the 'd' in 'door'
f	as the 'f' in 'feet'
j	as the 'j' in 'jar'
m	as the 'm' in 'me'
n	as the 'n' in 'net'
s	as the 's' in 'sin'
š	as the 'sh' in 'she'
t	as the 't' in 'toy'
v[2]	as the 'v' in 'vest'
y	as the 'y' in 'yes'
z	as the 'z' in 'zip'

There are three consonants in Persian, which do not exist in English. These consonants are:

x   as the 'ch' in the Scottish 'loch'.

---

[2] In Dari, this sound is mostly pronounced as *w*.

This consonant is pronounced at the back of the mouth, when the root of tongue makes a smooth contact with the end of the palate.

q   a guttural sound like a heavy French 'r'

This consonant is also pronounced at the back of the mouth, when the root of tongue makes a sudden contact with the end of the palate

ž   as the 'zh' in 'Zhivago' or the 'g' in 'mirage'

'   a glottal stop, which is pronounced in the throat and marks a break in the flow of speech.

The following consonants are slightly different from their English counterparts:

l   Persian l is pronounced in the front of the mouth, so it is similar to the 'l' in 'life', but not the 'l' in 'role'

k   It is similar to the English 'k' before and after 'ä, u, o' but it is palatalised with 'i, e, a' which is similar to the 'ck' in 'backyard'

r   similar to a trilled 'r' in English but never silent or diphthongised.

h as in the 'h' in 'hit'. It is never silent.

g like 'k' has two forms: it is like the 'g' in 'got' before or after 'ä, o, u', and similar to the 'g' in 'get' before or after 'a, e, i'

All Persian consonants can be doubled where they are always pronounced distinctly as in 'hot tea' but not in 'kettle'.

The pronunciation of Persian is easy and straightforward. Unlike in English, there is a consistency between pronunciation and spelling. Stress is generally on the last syllable of the word as in *näneväyi* 'bakery' and *hendväne* 'watermelon' where the stress is on the last syllable **yi** and ***ne***.

Persian alphabet الفبای فارسی

Although there is no need for Persian script to learn the language in this book, the alphabet is introduced here for the interested learners, and the sentenes in each lesson are shown both in transliteration and the script. The following table lists the names of all the letters of alphabet in Persian.

The shape of letters varies depending on whether the letter stands alone (independent), at the beginning of a word (initial), in the middle of a word (medial), or at the end of a word (final).

Final	Medial	Initial	Independent	Transliteration symbol
ـا		ا	ا	a
ـب	ـبـ	بـ	ب	b
ـپ	ـپو	پـ	پ	p
ـت	ـتـ	تـ	ت	t
ـث	ـثـ	ثـ	ث	s
ـج	ـجـ	جـ	ج	j
ـچ	ـچـ	چـ	چ	č
ـح	ـحـ	حـ	ح	h
ـخ	ـخـ	خـ	خ	x
ـد			د	d
ـذ			ذ	z

ـر			ر	r
ـز			ز	z
			ژ	ž
ـس	ـسـ	سـ	س	s
ـش	ـشـ	شـ	ش	š
ـص	ـصـ	صـ	ص	s
ـض	ـضـ	ضـ	ض	ž
ـط	ـطـ	طـ	ط	t
ـظ	ـظـ	ظـ	ظ	z
ـع	ـعـ	عـ	ع	ʻ
ـغ	ـغـ	غـ	غ	q
ـف	ـفـ	فـ	ف	f
ـق	ـقـ	قـ	ق	q
ـك	ـكـ	كـ	ك	k
ـگ	ـگـ	گـ	گ	g
ـل	ـلـ	لـ	ل	l
ـم	ـمـ	مـ	م	m
ـن	ـنـ	نـ	ن	n
ـه	ـهـ	هـ	ه	h
ـو			و	v
ـي	ـيـ	يـ	ي	y
		آ		ä

Guide for learning the lessons

- First, read the lesson by comparing the three lines for each phrase or sentence. The first line is in Persian, the second line is the literal translation of the sentence, and the third line is the English equivalent. By comparing these three lines, you will be able to learn the structure of the language and its differences and similarities with English.
- Read the new words and try to learn their meaning by practice. There are several ways to learn a new word. One way is to use flash cards. That is, you can write each word on a card and write the meaning on the back of the card. Then, practice remembering the meaning alternatively.
- Read the grammar section which is related to the materials being taught in the same lesson to understand the structor of the sentence.
- Finally, remember that the key to learn a new language is just practice and practice. You do not need to be a genius to learn a second language. You just need to practice more often.

Lesson 1 dars-e yek درس یک

Greetings	ahvälporsi احوالپرسی
Read these simple words for greeting, compliment, and politeness, and practice their pronunciation by using the transliteration.	

saläm hi	سلام	bale yes (informal)	بلی
xodähäfez good bye	خداحافظ	äre[3] yes (formal)	آره
bebaxšid excuse me	ببخشید	na no	نه
lotfan please	لطفا	motešakker-am[4] thank you	متشکرم
xeyli mamnun thank you very much	خیلی ممنون	bäše[5] OK, all right	باشه
xob[6] Ok, all right	خب	eškäl nadäre[7] does not matter	اشکال نداره

[3] bale.
[4] Tašakkor
[5] dorost ast
[6] xo. In Dari, the last consonant of the word is frequently deleted in the spoken style.
[7] parvä nadäre or farq ne-mi-konad

xäheš mikonam you welcome, that's Ok	خواهش می کنم	sobh bexeyr good morning	صبح بخیر
šab bexeyr good night	شب بخیر	'asr bexeyr good afternoon	عصر بخیر

Grammar hint: For more details on greetings in Persian, see **Greetings in Persian** in the grammar section.

Lesson 2   dars-e do   درس دو

Introduction   Mo'arrefi معرفی

Read these sentences in greetings and introduction, and learn about to be verbs in Persian.

---

saläm, šomä četor **hast-in**[8]?   سلام شما چطور هستین؟
hi you how are-you?
Hi. How are you?

xeyli mamnun[9]. man xub **hast-am**.   خیلی ممنون. من خوب هستم.
many thanks .I fine am-I
Thank you very much. I am fine.

esm[10]-etun či hast?   اسم تون چی هست؟
name-your what is
What is your name?

esm-am därä hast.   اسم ام دارا هست.
name-my Dara is
My name is Dara.

---

[8] In Dari, *hast* is usually pronounced and written as *ast*.
[9] besyär tašakkor
[10] näm

esm-e dust-etun či **hast**? اسم دوست تون چی هست؟
name of friend-your what is
What is your friend's name?

esm-e un maryam **hast**. اسم اون مریم هست.
name of her Maryam is
Her name is Maryam.

saläm maryam xošbax-am. سلام مریم. خوشبختم.
hi Maryam lucky am
Hi Maryam. Nice to meet you.

man ham hamintor. من هم همینطور.
I also the same
Me too.

Grammar hint: As we see in the above sentences, the words in bold are *to be* (copula) verbs. To see more explanation on these verbs, refer to **Copul**a in the grammar section.

New words		
Persian	**English**	فارسی
saläm	hi	سلام
šomä	you (Plural)	شما
četor	how	چطور
hast-am, hast-i, hast	I am, you are (singular), he/she/it is	هستم،

		هستی، هست
hast-im, hast-id-hast-and	we are, you are (plural), they are	هستیم، هستید، هستند
man	I	من
xub	good	خوب
mamnun	thanks	ممنون
dust	friend	دوست
esm	name	اسم
am, et, eš, emun, etun, ešun	my, your, his/her/its, our, your, their	ام، ات، اش، امون، اتون، اشون
či	what	چی
un	he, she, it	اون

Lesson 3   darse se   درس سه

Languages   zabänhä   زبانها
In this lesson, you will learn a simple conversation about language and the related terms.

šomä če **zabän**[11]-i sohbat mi-kon-in[12]?
you what language speak
What language do you speak?
شما چه زبانی صحبت می کنید؟

man **färsi** sohbat mi-kon-am.
I   Farsi speak.
I speak Farsi.
من فارسی صحبت می کنم.

šomä **ingilisi** mi-fahm-in?
you English understand
Do you understand English?
شما انگلیسی می فهمین؟

---

[11] lesän
[12] gap mi-zan-in

na, man **ingilisi** ne-mi-fahm-am.
no, I   English   do not understand
No, I do not understand English.

نه من انگلیسی نمی فهمم.

lotfan yaväš[13] sohbat be-kon-in.
please slow   do speak
Please speak slowly.

لطفا یواش صحبت بکنین.

bäše un **rä** tekrär mi-kon-am[14].
Ok   it OM[15] repeat do   I
Ok, I will repeat it.

باشه آن را تکرار می کنم.

man **ma'ni** -ye un **rä** ne-midän-am
I   meaning of it OM   do not know
I do not know its meaning.

من معنی آن را نمی دانم.

---

[13] ähesta
[14] There are differences in pronounciation between spoken and written styles of Persian. The words in the spoken style are usually shortened or attached together. For example, in conversation *un rä* becomes *uno*. For the sake of regularity and simplicity of learning, in this book the written style has been used as much as possible.
[15] Object marker

Grammar hint: The words in bold are objects. To see more on objects in Persian, refer to **Object** in the grammar section.

The word rä is an object marker. Refer to **Object marker** in the grammar section.

New words		
Persian	**English**	فارسی
zabän	language	زبان
sohbat mi-kon-in	you speak	صحبت می کنین
ingilisi	English	انگلیسی
mi-fahm-in	you understand	می فهمین
na	no	نه
ne-mi-fahm-am	I do not understand	نمی فهمم
yaväš	slowly	یواش
bäše	Ok	باشه
rä	marker for definite object	را
tekrär mi-kon-am	I repeat	تکرار می کنم
ma'ni	meaning	معنی
(y)e	marker for possession	/16
ne-midän-am	I do not know	نمی دانم

---

[16] This possessive marker does not appear in the script and is used only for teaching purposes in primary school textbooks.

Lesson 4   darse čähär   درس چهار

Feelings   ehsäsät   احساسات
This lesson introduces basic words and phrases about expressing of feelings and emotions.

saläm, häl-etun   četor hast?
Hi   condition-your how   is
Hi. How are you?
سلام حالتون چطور هست؟

man xub   hast-am.
I   good   am
I am good.
من خوب هستم.

to az čizi närähat[17] hast-i?
you from something upset   are-you
Are you upset about something?
تو از چیزی ناراحت هستی؟

---

[17] xafa

28

na bar aks, **man** xeyli xošhäl hast-am.
no opposite I   very happy   am
No, on the opposite, I am very happy.

نه برعکس من خیلی خوشحال هستم.

pedar-etun   mariz[18] hast?
father-your   sick   is
Is your father sick?

پدرتون مریض هست؟

na **un**   xeyli kär kärd va xaste hast
no, he very work did and tired   is
No, he worked a lot and is tired.

نه اون خیلی کار کرد و خسته هست.

čerä šomä asabäni[19] hast-in?
why you   angry   are-you
Why are you angry?

چرا شما عصبانی هستین؟

---

[18] näjur
[19] qahr

man asabäni nist-am. faqat negarän hast-am

I   angry am-not. just worried am-I

I am not angry. I am just worried.

من عصبانی نیستم. فقط نگران هستم.

Grammar hint: Words like *man, šomä, pedar-etun* are subjects (Refer to No.12 in the grammar section).

Words like *čerä* are called question words (Refer to **Interrogatives** in the grammar section).

New words		
Persian	**English**	فارسی
häl	condition	حال
xub	good	خوب
to	you (singular)	تو
närähat	upset	ناراحت
xošhäl	happy	خوشحال
mariz	sick	مریض
xaste	tired	خسته
asabäni	angry	عصبانی
negarän	worried	نگران

Lesson 5   darse panj   درس پنج

Personal details   joz'iyäte šaxsi   جزئیات شخصی
In this lesson, you will learn how to ask about simple personal details like name, age and nationality.

esm-etun či **hast**?
name-your what is
What is your name?
اسمتون چی هست؟

esm-am ali ahmadi **hast**
name-my ali ahmadi is
My name is Ali Ahmadi.
اسمم علی احمدی هست.

šomä čand säl **där-in**?
you how many year have-you
How old are you?
شما چند سال دارین؟

man bist šal **där-am**
I twenty year have-I
I am twenty years old.
من بیست سال دارم.

šomä kojä-yi **hast-in?**[20]

you where-from are-you

Where are you from?

شما کجائی هستین؟

man irän-i **hast-am**

I Iranian am

I am Iranian.

من ایرانی هستم.

šoql-etun či **hast?**

job-your what is

What is your job?

شغل تون چی هست؟

man kärmand[21] **hast-am**

I public servant am

I am a government employee.

من کارمند هستم.

Grammar hint: Words like *där* and *hast* are verbs (Refer to **Verb** in the grammar section).

---

[20] šomä az kojä ast-in?
[21] ma'mur

New words		
Persian	**English**	**فارسی**
čand	how many, how much	چند
säl	year	سال
där-in	you have	دارین
kojä-yi	where from	کجائی
iräni	Iranian	ایرانی
šoql	job	شغل
kärmand	employee	کارمند

Grammar hint: To show belonging to a place, we add /i/ at the end of the place name. For example, if we add /i/ to Iran, it means Iranian. Here is the list of some country names in Persian:

Persian	English	فارسی	Persian	English	فارسی
ämrika	America	آمریکا	ämrika-i	American	آمریکایی
ostäräliyä	Australia	استرالیا	ostäräliyä-i	Australian	استرالیایی
otriš[22]	Austria	اتریش	otriš-i[23]	Austrian	اتریشی
engilis	English	انگلیس	engilis-i	English	انگلیسی
älmän[24]	Germany	آلمان	älmän-i	German	آلمانی
faränese	France	فرانسه	faränese-vi[25]	French	فرانسوی
itäliyä	Italy	ایتالیا	itäliyä-yi	Italian	ایتالیایی
norvež[26]	Norway	نروژ	norvež-i	Norwegian	نروژی
hend	India	هند	hend-i	Indian	هندی
čin	China	چین	čin-i	Chinese	چینی
žäpon	Japan	ژاپن	žäpon-i	Japanise	ژاپنی
Mesr	Egypt	مصر	mesr-i	Egyptian	مصری
Arabestän	Saudi Arabian	عربستان	Arabestän-i	Saudi Arabian	عربستانی
Suriye	Syria	سوریه	Sur-i	Syrian	سوری

---

[22] ästeriyä
[23] ästeriyäyi
[24] germani
[25] If a country name ends in a vowel, we add –yi and if it ends in a consonant, we add –i. There are some exceptions like in this one where –vi is attached to Faränese.
[26] norwey

Lesson 6   darse šeš   درس شش

Occupations   šoqlhä   شغل ها

In this lesson, you will learn about the names of different jobs.

šoql-e šomä či **hast**?

job-of you what it

What is your job?

شغل شما چی هست؟

man mo'allem **hast-am**

I teacher am

I am a teacher.

من معلم هستم.

šomä dar kojä **kär mi-kon-in**?

you in where work do –you

Where do you work?

شما در کجا کار می کنین؟

man dar madrese[27] **kär mi-kon-am**

I in school work do-I

I work in a school.

من در مدرسه کار می کنم.

---

[27] maktab

šomä či **kär mi-kon-in**
you what work do-you
What do you do?
شما چکار می کنین؟

man parastär[28] **hast-am**.
I nurse am
I am a nurse.
من پرستار هستم.

man dar bimärestän[29] **kär mi-kon-am**
I in hospital work do-I
I work in a hospital.
من در بیمارستان کار می کنم.

hamsar-etun ham **kär mi-kon-ad**?
partner-your also work do-s/he
Does your partner work too?
همسرتان هم کار می کند؟

---

[28] nars
[29] šafäxäna

na, un bikär **hast**

no, he without work is

No, he is unemployed.

نه. اون بیکار هست.

Grammar hint: Verbs like *hast* and *kär mikonam* are in present tense (Refer to **Present tens**e in the grammar section).

New words		
Persian	**English**	**فارسی**
kär mi-kon-in	you work	کار می کنین
či	what	چه
kojä	where	کجا
dar	in, at	در
madrese	school	مدرسه
hamsar	partner	همسر
ham	also	هم
bikär	unemployed	بیکار

jobs		
mo'allem	teacher	معلم
šägerd	student	شاگرد
jahängard	tourist	جهانگرد
mohandes[30]	engineer	مهندس
täjer	businessman	تاجر
ränande[31]	driver	راننده
vakil	lawyer	وکیل
kärmand	office worker	کارمند
kärgar[32]	labourer	کارگر
xänedär[33]	housewife	خانه دار

---

[30] injiniyar
[31] motarwän, deräywar
[32] amala
[33] zane xäna

Lesson 7   darse haft   درس هفت

Family   xänavade   خانواده
In this lesson, you will learn terms about family and kinship.

mehrän, šomä[34] mota'ahhel hast-**in**?

Mehran, you married are-you

Are you married mehran?

مهران، شما متاهل هستین؟

bale man do tä bačče[35] där-**am**

yes I two child have-I

Yes, I have two children.

بله. من دو تا بچه دارم.

šomä či farid?

you what Farid

What about you Farid?

شما چی، فرید؟

---

[34] The pronoun for second person singular is *to* (you.singular) but it is used to address the close friends and relatives and children. For other people, the pronoun for second person plural *šomä* is used for politeness.

[35] tefel: *bačča* in Dari means son.

man mota'ahhel nist-**am** vali nämzad där-**am**.
I married am-not but fiancé have-I
I am not married but I have a fiancé.
من متاهل نیستم ولی نامزد دارم.

šomä key ezdeväj mi-kon-**in**?
you when marriage do-you
When are you getting married?
شما کی ازدواج می کنین؟

mä šäyad mäh-e ba'd ezdevaj be-kon-**im**
we may month of next marriage do-we
We may marry next month.
ما شاید ماه بعد ازدواج بکنیم.

mehrän šomä čand tä bačče där-**in**?
Mehran you how many child have-you
How many children do you have, Mehran?
مهران، شما چند تا بچه دارین؟

man do tä pesar[36] va se tä doxtar där-**am**
I two son and three daughter have-I
I have two sons and three daughters.
من دو تا پسر و سه تا دختر دارم.

farid, šomä čand tä xähar[37] va barädar där-**in**?
Farid, you how many sister and brother have-you
How many brothers and sisters do you have, Farid?
فرید، شما چند تا خواهر و برادر دارین؟

man čähär tä xähar va panj tä barädar där-**am**
I four sister and five brother have-I
I have four sisters and five brothers.
من چهار تا خواهر و پنج تا برادر دارم.

Grammar hint: Words like im, in, am are called verb suffixes (Refer to **Suffixes** in the grammar section).

---

[36] bačče
[37] xwähar

New words

Persian	English	فارسی
mota'ahhel	married	متاهل
bačče	child	بچه
där	to have	دار
tä	classifier for number	تا
hanuz	yet	هنوز
ezdeväj kon	to marry	ازدواج کن
vali	but	ولی
nämzad	fiancé	نامزد
key	when	کی
mäh	month	ماه
ba'd	next	بعد
va	and	و

Numbers

Read and learn these numbers in Persian:

yek	1	۱	yäzdah	11	۱۱	thirty	si	30	۳۰
do	2	۲	daväzdah	12	۱۲	forty	čehel	40	۴۰
se	3	۳	sizdah	13	۱۳	fifty	panjäh	50	۵۰
čähär	4	۴	čähärdah	14	۱۴	sixty	šast	60	۶۰
panj	5	۵	punzdah	15	۱۵	seventy	haftäd	70	۷۰
šeš	6	۶	sänzdah	16	۱۶	eigthy	haštäd	80	۸۰
haft	7	۷	hefdah	17	۱۷	ninety	navad	90	۹۰
hašt	8	۸	hejdah	18	۱۸	hundered	sad	100	۱۰۰
noh	9	۹	nuzdah	19	۱۹	thusand	hezär	1000	۱۰۰۰
dah	10	۱۰	bist	20	۲۰	milion	melyon	1000000	۱۰۰۰۰۰۰

Learn these words about kinship:

šohar	huband	شوهر
zan	wife	زن
doxtar	daughter	دختر
pesar	son, boy	پسر
pedar	father	پدر

mädar	mother	مادر
xähar	sister, girl	خواهر
barädar	brother	برادر
pedar bozorg[38]	grand father	پدر بزرگ
mädar bozorg[39]	grand mother	مادر بزرگ
amme	aunt (paternal)	عمه
amu[40]	uncle (paternal)	عمو
xäle	aunt (maternal)	خاله
däyi[41]	uncle (maternal)	دایی
arus	bride, daughter in law	عروس
dämäd	groom, son in law	داماد

---

[38] pedar kalän
[39] mädar kalän
[40] käkä
[41] mämä

Lesson 8   darse hašt   درس هشت

Travel   mosäferat   مسافرت

In this lesson, you will learn about travel and getting around.

saläm, **miše** az šomä yek so'äl be-kon-am?

Hi possibly from you one question do-I

Hi. Can I ask you a question?

سلام، میشه از شما یک سئوال بکنم؟

bale hatman.

yes, sure.

Yes, sure.

بله. حتما.

man četor mi-tavän-am be markaz-e šahr[42] **be-rav-am**?

I how can-I to centre of city go-I

How can I go to the downtown?

من چطور می توانم به مرکز شهر بروم.

---

[42] šär

šomä mi-tavän-in injä yek täksi be-gir-in.

you can here taxi take-you

You can take a taxi here.

شما می توانین اینجا یک تاکسی بگیرین.

mersi[43], mi-dän-in keräye tä unjä čeqadr mi-šav-ad?
thanks, know-you fare to there how much become-it
Thanks, do you know how much the fare is to there?

مرسی می دانین کرایه تا اونجا چقدر می شود؟

fekr mi-kon-am hodude hezär[44] toman mi-šav-ad
think do-I about thousand Toman become-it
I think it is about one thousand Toman.

فکر می کنم حدود هزار تومان می شود.

pas man bäyad injä savär be-šav-am[45]?
so, I should here on foot become-I
So, I should get on (the taxi) here?

پس من باید اینجا سوار بشوم؟

---

[43] tašakkor
[44] yak hazär
[45] päyin mišawam

bale va bäyad dar xiyäbän-e enqeläb piyäde be-šav-in
Yes and should in street of Enghelab on foot become-you
Yes, and you should get off in Enghelab Street.

بله و باید در خیابان انقلاب پیاده بشوین.

Grammar hint:

The word *miše* is a short form of the verb *mišavad* (i.e. is it possible?)

The second verb in the sentence (like *be-rav-am*) comes with the prefix *be-* (Refer to **Prefix be** and **Second Verb** in the grammar section).

New words		
Persian	**English**	فارسی
miše	Is it possible?	میشه
so'al kon	to ask	سئوال کن
hatman	sure	حتما
četor	how	چطور
tavän	can	توان
markaz	centre	مرکز
šahr	city	شهر
rav	to go	رو
injä	there	اینجا
gir	To get	گیر
bebaxšin	excuse me	ببخشین
xäh	to want	خواه
keräye	fare	کرایه
dän	To know	دان
Fekr kon	To think	فکر کن
hodude	about	حدود

hezär	thousand	هزار
toman	Iranian currency	تومان
šav	to become	شو
savär šav	to get on	سوار شو
piyäde šav	to get off	پیاده شو
mersi	thanks	مرسی

Lesson 9   darse noh   درس نه

Weather   havä   هوا
In this lesson, you will learn about weather condition and days of the week.

mi-dän-in emruz če ruz-i hast?

you know today what day is

Do you know what day is today?

می دانین امروز چه روزی هست؟

bale emruz pajšanbe hast.

yes today Thursday is

Yes, today is Thursday.

بله امروز پنج شنبه هست.

rästi diruz havä xeyli sard bud.

by the way, yesterday weather very cold was

By the way. yesterday, it was very cold.

راستی دیروز هوا خیلی سرد بود.

vali farad[46] havä äftäbi va garm hast

but tomorrow weather sunny and warm is

But tomorrow, it is sunny and warm.

ولی فردا هوا آفتابی و گرم هست.

emsäl bärän[47] ziyäd hast.

this year rain a lot is

This year, there is a lot of rain.

امسال باران زیاد هست.

mäh-e qabl barf-e ziyädi ämad

month-of previous snow a lot came

Last month, there was a lot of snow.

ماه قبل برف زیادی آمد.

Grammar hint: The words after *če* are followed by the vowel *i*, as in *če ruz-i* (Refer to **Word če** in the grammar section).

---

[46] sabäh
[47] bäreš

related words		
Persian	**English**	فارسی
ruz	day	روز
emruz	today	امروز
diruz	yesterday	دیروز
fardä	tomorrow	فردا
hafte	week	هفته
mäh	month	ماه
säl	year	سال
emsäl	this year	امسال
pärsäl	last year	پارسال
säl-e äyande	next year	سال آینده
barf	snow	برف
bärän	rain	باران
bäd[48]	wind	باد
tagarg[49]	hail	تگرگ
yax	ice	یخ
äb	water	آب
abr	cloud	ابر
sard	cold	سرد
garm	warm	گرم
havä	weather	هوا

---

[48] šamäl
[49] žala

Lesson 10   darse dah   درس ده

At the restaurant   dar resturän   در رستوران
In this lesson, you will learn about communication in the restaurant, ordering a meal and paying the bill.

saläm. mä yek **miz-e do nafar-e** mi-xäh-im
hi. we one table-of tow people want-we
Hi. We want a table for two.
سلام. ما یک میز دو نفره می خواهیم.

befarmäyin. injä yek **miz-e do nafar-e** kenär-e pajare[50] hast.
PP. here a table of two people beside window is
Here you are. Here is a table for two beside the window.
بفرمائین. اینجا یک میز دو نفره کنار پنجره هست.

xeyli mamnun. šomä če qazä-hä-yi där-in?
very thanks. you what foods have-you
Thanks a lot. What food do you have?
خیلی ممنون. شما چه غذاهایی دارین؟

---

[50] kelkin

befarmäyin. in **list[51]-e qazä-hä-ye mä** hast.
PP. this list of foods of we is
Here you are. This is our menu.
بفرمائین. این لیست غذاهای ما هست.

xob. miše mä alän sefäreš[52] be-dah-im?
Ok. can we now order give-we
Ok. Can we order now?
خوب. میشه ما الان سفارش بدهیم؟

bale hatman. či meyl där-in?
yes sure   what desire have-you
Yes, sure. What would you like?
بله حتما. چی میل دارین؟

baräye mä yek čelo kabäb va yek juje kabäb bi-yävar-in.
for we one rice kebab and one chicken kebab bring-you
Bring us one kebab with rice and one chicken kebab.
برای ما یک چلوکباب و یک جوجه کباب بیاورید.

---

[51] meno
[52] farmäyeš

nušābe či mi-xäh-in?
drink what want-you
What drink do you want?
نوشابه چی می خواهید؟

man faqat äb mi-xor-am vali dust-am äb mive mi-xor-ad.
I only water eat-I but friend-my water fruit eats
I will just have water but my friend will have fruit juice.
من فقط آب می خورم ولی دوستم آب میوه می خورد.

bäše. avval baräye šomä nän[53] va sabzi[54] mi-ävar-im.
Ok. first for you bread and vegetable bring-we
Ok. First I will bring you some bread and vegetable.
باشه. اول برای شما نان و سبزی می آوریم.

befarmäyin in ham qäzä-ye šomä. nuše jän
PP this also food of you. pleasant to your body
Here you are. Here is your meal. Bona petit.
بفرمائین. این هم غذای شما. نوش جان.

---

[53] näne xošk
[54] tarkäri

bebaxšin. miše surat hesäb[55] rä biy-ävar-in?
excuse-you. can face count OM bring-you
Excuse me, can you bring the bill please?

ببخشید. میشه صورت حساب را بیاورید؟

befarfäyin. dah hezär toman mi-šav-ad. qazä xub bud?
RP. ten thousand toman becomes. food good was
Here you are. It is ten thousand tomans. Was the food good?

بفرمائین. ده هزار تومن می شود. غذا خوب بود؟

bale. xeyli xošmaze[56] bud.
yes. very tasty was.
Yes, it was very delicious.

بله. خیلی خوشمزه بود.

Grammar hint: The phrases in bold are called Possessive phrases (Refer to **Possession** in the grammar section).

related words		
Persian	English	فارسی
miz	table	میز
nafar	person	نفر
kenär	beside	کنار
panjare	window	پنجره
qazä	food	غذا
liste qazä	menu	لیست غذا

---

[55] bel
[56] mazadär

miše	is it possible?	میشه
sefäreš dah	to order	سفارش ده
alän	now	الان
meyl där	to like	میل دار
čelo kabä	rice & kebab	چلو کباب
juje kabäb	chicken & rice	جوجه کباب
nušäbe	drink	نوشابه
faqat	only	فقط
äb mive	fruit juice	آب میوه
avval	first	اول
nän	bread	نان
sabzi	vegetable	سبزی
ävar	to bring	آور
nuše jän	Bona petit	نوش جان
surat hesäb	bill	صورت حساب
xošmaze	tasty	خوشمزه

Lesson 11   darse yäzdah   درس یازده

Booking hotel   reserve hotel   رزرو هتل

In this lesson, you will learn about booking accommodation, asking for fare and filling the forms.

saläm, aqä

hello, Mr.

Hello sir.

سلام آقا.

saläm, **befarmäyin**[57]

Hello, PP

hello, how can I help you?

سلام بفرمائین.

man mi-xäh-am yek otäq rezerv be-kon-am

I want-I one room reserve do-I

I want to book a room.

من می خواهم یک اتاق رزرو بکنم.

---

[57] politeness phrase

čand xäbe va baräye čand šab?

how many bed and for how many night

How many beds and for how many nights?

چند خوابه و برای چند شب؟

baräye yek šab. keräye-ye har šab čeqadr mi-šav-ad?

for one night. rent of each night how much become-it

For one night. How much is the fare per night?

برای یک شب. کرایه هر شب چقدر می شود؟

har šab dah hezär toman mi-šav-ad.

each night ten thousand toman become-it

Each night is 10 thousand Toman.

هر شب ده هزار تومن می شود.

bäše. man otäq rä baräye fardä šab mi-xäh-am.

Ok. I room OM for tomorrow night want-I

I want the room for tomorrow night.

باشه. من اتاق را برای فردا شب می خواهم.

bäše. Lotfan in form rä por be-kon-in[58]

Ok. Please this form OM fill do-you

Ok. Please fill in this form.

باشه. لطفا این فرم را پر کنین.

Grammar hint: The word *befarmäyin* is a politeness word and has different meanings (Refer to **Politeness** in the grammar section).

Related words		
yek xäbe	single bed	یک خوابه
do xäbe	double bed	دو خوابه
xäli	vacant	خالی
bey'äne	deposit	بیعانه
barq	electricity	برق
šir-e äb	water tap	شیر آب
duš	shower	دوش
dast šuyi	bathroom	دست شویی
pazireš	reception	پذیرش
kelid	key	کلید
patu	blanket	پتو
boxari	heater	بخاری
kuler	cooler	کولر
New words		
Persian	**English**	فارسی
otäq	room	اتاق
rezerv kon	to book	رزرو کن
baräye	for	برای
keräye	rent, fare	کرایه
injä	here	اینجا
äy	to come	آی
por kon	to fill	پر کن

---

[58] xäna pori kon-in

Lesson 12   darse daväzdah   درس دوازده

Time and date   vaqt va tärix   وقت و تاریخ
In this lesson, you will learn about time and date.

bebaxšid, sä'at čand[59] hast?
excuse-you, time how much is
Excuse me, what time is it?
ببخشید، ساعت چند هست؟

sä'at yek o dah daqiqe hast
time one and ten minute is
It is ten past one.
ساعت یک و ده دقیقه هست.

otubus-e[60] in xat key mi-äy-ad?
bus of this route when come-it
When does the bus for this route arrive?
اتوبوس این خط کی می آید؟

---

[59] čand baja
[60] sarwis

ba'd az nim sä'at ya'ni sä'at-e panj o nim
after half hour, meaning time five and half
After half an hour. That is, at five thirsty.
بعد از نیم ساعت. یعنی ساعت پنج و نیم.

in qatär[61] key harekat mi-kon-ad?
this train when move do-it
When does this train leave?
این قطار کی حرکت می کند؟

hodude punzdah daqiqe be do
around hour fifteen minute to two
Around fifteen minutes to two.
حدود پانزده دقیقه به دو

emruz če ruz-i az hafte hast?
today what day of week is
What day of the week is today?
امروز چه روزی از هفته هست؟

---

[61] rayl

emruz yekšanbe hast.

today Sunday is

Today is Sunday.

امروز یکشنبه هست

Grammar hint: Words in bold are called subject (Refer to **Subject** in the grammar section).

New words		
Persian	**English**	**فارسی**
sä'at	time, hour, watch	ساعت
daqiqe	minute	دقیقه
o (va)	and	و
otubus	bus	اتوبوس
nim	half	نیم
qatär	train	قطار
harekat kon	to depart	حرکت کن
hafte	week	هفته
ruz	day	روز
šanbe	Saturday	شنبه
yekšanbe	Sunday	یکشنبه
došanbe	Monday	دوشنبه
sešanbe	Tuesday	سه شنبه
čähäršanbe	Wednesday	چهار شنبه
panjšanbe	Thursday	پنج شنبه
jom'e	Friday	جمعه

Lesson 13   darse sizdah   درس سیزده

Daily routines   kärhäye ruzmarre   کارهای روزمره
In this lesson, you will learn to talk about daily activities, using simple phrases.

man har šab sä'at-e noh mi-xäb-am[62].
I each night hour of nine sleep-I
I sleep at nine o'clock every night.
من هر شب ساعت نه می خوابم.

čon sobh zud **bidär mi-šav-am**[63] va be edäre mi-rav-am.
because morning soon awake become-I and to office go-I
Because I wake up early morning and go to the office.
چون صبح زود بیدار می شوم و به اداره می روم.

har šab qabl az xäb **duš mi-gir-am**[64].
each night before sleep shower take-I
I take shower every night before bed.
هر شب قبل از خواب دوش می گیرم.

---

[62] xwäb mišawäm
[63] mixizam
[64] šäwer mikonam

sä'at-e panj-e sobh **bidär mi-šav-am**.
hour of five of morning awake become-I
I wake up at five o'clock in the morning.
ساعت پنج صبح بیدار می شوم.

surat-am rä mi-šur-am va mesväk[65] mi-zan-am.
face-my OM wash-I and brush hit-I
I wash my face and brush my teeth.
صورتم را می شورم و مسواک می زنم.

man hič vaqt sobhäne[66] ne-mixor-am.
I never breakfast no east-I
I never eat breakfast.
من هیچ وقت صبحانه نمی خورم.

har ruz sobh sä'at-e hašt be edäre mi-rav-am.
every day morning hour of eight to office go-I
I go to the office eight o'clock every morning.
هر روز صبح ساعت هشت به اداره می روم.

---

[65] beräš
[66] čäye sobh

sä'at-e panj-e asr[67] az edäre be xäne bar-mi-gard-am.
hour of five of afternoon from office to home come back-I
I return home from office at five o'clock in the afternoon.
ساعت پنج عصر از اداره به خانه بر می گردم.

ba'd yek sä'at televiziyon negäh mi-kon-am
then one hour TV look-do-I
Then, I watch TV for one hour.
بعد یک ساعت تلویزیون نگاه می کنم.

ba'd šam mi-xor-am va yek sä'at ketäb mi-xän-am
then dinner eat-I and one hour book read-I
Then, I eat dinner and read a book for an hour.
بعد شام می خورم و یک ساعت کتاب می خوانم.

Grammar hint: Verbs in bold are called compound verb (Refer to **Compound verbs** in the grammar section).

New words		
Persian	**English**	فارسی
har	every, each	هر
šab	night	شب
xäb	to sleep	خواب
čon	because	چون
bidär šav	to wake up	بیدار شو
edäre	office	اداره

---

[67] digar

qabl	before	قبل
duš gir	to take shower	دوش گیر
ba'd	then	بعد
surat	face	صورت
šur	to wash	شور
mesväk zan	to brush	مسواک زن
sobhäne	breakfast	صبحانه
hič vaqt	never	هیچ وقت
bar gard	to return	برگرد
asr	afternoon	عصر

Lesson 14 darse čahärdah درس چهارده

At the bank   dar bank   در بانک
In this lesson, you will learn about simple transactions, changing money, depositing money and signing papers.

saläm xänom, injä bank-e melli hast?
hello madam, here bank of national is
Hello. Madam, is this the national bank?
سلام خانم. اینجا بانک ملی هست؟

bale. befarmäyin.
yes. PP
Yes, How can I help you?
بله بفرمایین؟

man **mi-xäh-am** meqdäri dolär be toman[68] tabdil **be-kon-am**.
I want some dollar to Toman change do-I
I want to change some dollars into Tomans.
من می خواهم مقداری دلار به تومان تبدیل بکنم.

---

[68] paseye afqäni

dollar-etun čeqadr hast?
dollar-your how much is
How much is your dollars?
دلارتون چقدر هست؟

faqat, hezär dollar där-am. nerx-e dolär čand hast?
only thousand dollar have-I. rate of dollar what is
I have Just one thousand dollars. What is the rate of dollar?
فقط هزار دلار دارم. نرخ دلار چند هست؟

emruz har dolär nohsad toman hast.
today each dollar nine hindered Toman is
Today, each dollar is nine hindered Tomans.
امروز هر دلار نه صد تومان هست.

pas loftan in rä baräye man tabdil be-kon-in.
so please this OM for me change do-you
So, please change this for me.
پس لطفا این را برای من تبدیل بکنید.

xob. pas loftan injä rä emzä be-kon-in.
Ok. so please here OM sign do-you
Ok. Then, please sign here.
خب. پس لطفا اینجا را امضا بکنید.

man **mi-xäh-am** in pul[69] rä be hesäb-am **be-gozär-am**[70]

I want-I this money OM to account-my put-I

I want to deposit this money in my account.

من می خواهم این پول را به حسابم بگذارم.

bäše. Lotfan daftarče-ye hesäb-etun rä be man be-dah-in.

Ok. please notebook of account-your OM to me give-you

Ok. Please give me your account book.

باشه. لطفا دفترچه حسابتون را به من بدهید.

Grammar hint: When there are two verbs in the sentence, the second verb comes with be- (Refer to **Second Verb** in the grammar section).

New words		
Persian	English	فارسی
bank-e melli	national bank	بانک ملی
meqdäri	some	مقداری
tabdil kon	to exchange	تبدیل کن
faqat	only	فقط
nerx	rate	نرخ
emzä kon	to sign	امضا کن
pul	money	پول
hesäb	account	حساب
gozär	to put	گذار
daftarče-ye hesäb	account book	دفترچه حساب

---

[69] paysa
[70] bemänam

Lesson 15   darse pänzdah   درس پانزده

At the chemist   dar däruxäne   در داروخانه
In this lesson, you will learn about getting medicine from chemist and asking about the instructions for using it.

saläm. man yek qatre-ye češm va yek baste qors[71] mi-xäh-am.
hi. I one drop of eye and one pack of tablet want-I
Hi. I want an eye drop and a pack of tablet.

سلام من یک قطره چشم و یک بسته قرص می خواهم

šomä **baräye** in qatre nosxe läzem[72] där-in
you for this drop prescription need have-you
You need a prescription for the drop.

شما برای این قطره نسخه لازم دارید.

bäše. mi-tavän-in faqat qors rä be man be-dah-in?
Ok. can-you just tablet to me give-you
Ok. Can you give me just the tablet?

باشه می توانید فقط قرص را به من بدهید؟

---

[71] guli
[72] zarurat

bale, befarmäyin, in qors mosakken hast.
yes, PP, this tablet painkiller is
Yes. Here you are. This tablet is a painkiller.
بله. بفرمایین. این قرص مسکن هست.

čand bär bäyad **az** in qors be-xor-am?
how may time should from this tablet eat-I
How many times should I take this tablet?
چند بار باید از این قرص بخورم؟

čähär bär **dar** ruz. har šiš sä'at yek qors be-xor-in
four time in day. each six hour one tablet eat-you
Four times a day. Take one tablet every six hours.
چهار بار در روز. هر شش ساعت یک قرص بخورید.

Grammar hint: The words in bold are called prepositions (Refer to **Prepositions** in the grammar section).

New words		
Persian	**English**	فارسی
däruxäne	chemist, drugstore	داروخانه
baste	pack	بسته
qors	tablet	قرص
däru	medicine	دارو
nosxe	prescription	نسخه
läzem där	to need	لازم دار
dige	else	دیگه
mosakken	painkiller	مسکن

bär	time	بار
aväreze jänebi	side effects	عوارض جانبی
ma'mulan	usually	معمولا
šäyad	may be	شاید
xäbävar	drowsy	خواب اور

Lesson 16   darse šänzdah   درس شانزده

At doctor's surgery   dar matabbe doctor   در مطب دکتر
In this lesson, you will learn about visiting doctors and telling about your state of health, and the terms about body parts, and different symptoms and illnesses.

mariz: bebaxšin, miše doktor rä be-bin-am?
patient excuse me, is it possible doctor see-I
Patient: excuse me, can I see the doctor?
مریض ببخشید میشه دکتر را ببینم.

monši: bale. vali bäyad yek sä'at sabr be-kon-in
receptionist: yes, but should one hour wait do-you
Receptionist: Yes, but you should wait an hour.
بله اما باید یک ساعت صبر کنید.

doktor: saläm, befarmäyin. moškel či hast[73]?
doctor: hi. PP. problem is what
Doctor: Hi. How can I help you? What is the problem?
دکتر: سلام. بفرمایین. مشکل چی هست؟

äqäye doktor[74], šekam-am dard mi-kon-ad

---
[73] či taklif därin?

Mr doctor, tummy-my ache do-it

Doctor, my tummy aches.

آقای دکتر، شکمم درد می کند.

Sorfe ham där-in?

cough also have-you

Do you have a cough too?

سرفه هم دارید؟

bale, sorfe mi-kon-am va galu dard ham där-am

yes, cough do-I and throat pain also have-I

Yes, I cough and I have sore throat as well.

بله سرفه می کنم و گلو درد هم دارم.

bäše eyb nadäre man alän šomä rä mo'äyene mi-kon-am

Ok. fault no have-it, I now you examine-do I

Ok. No problem. I will give examine you know.

باشه. عیب نداره. من الان شما را معاینه می کنم.

Grammar hint: The verb *nadär-e* is the colloquial form for *nadär-ad* (Refer to **Colloquial forms** in the grammar section).

Body parts		
Persian	English	فارسی

[74] däktar säheb

angošt	finger	انگشت
bäzu	arm	بازو
bini	nose	بینی
čane	chin	چانه
češm	eye	چشم
dahän	mouth	دهان
dandän	tooth	دندان
dast	hand	دست
gardan	neck	گردن
guš	ear	گوش
lab	lip	لب
mu	hair	مو
näxon	nail	ناخن
pä	foot	پا
šäne	shoulder	شانه
sar	head	سر
sine	chest	سینه
surat	face	صورت
zänu	knee	زانو

New words		
Persian	**English**	فارسی
moškel	problem	مشکل
dard kon	to ache	درد کن
sar dard	head ache	سر درد
sar jige	dizziness	سرگیجه
gors	tablet	قرص
mosakken	sedative	مسکن
eyb nadäre	it does not matter	عیب نداره
alän	now	الان
däru	medicine	دارو

Lesson 17   darse hefdah   درس هفده

At the supermarket dar furušgäh در فروشگاه

In this lesson, you will learn about communication in the shop and buying grocery items.

forušande[75]: befarmäyin.

shopkeeper: PP

Shopkeeper: How can I help you?

فروشنده: بفرمایین؟

moštari: šomä bätri där-in?

customer: you battery have-you

Customer: Do you have battery?

مشتری: شما باطری دارین؟

bale. če no' bätri mi-xäh-in

yes. what type battery want-you

Yes, what type of battery do you want?

بله. چه نوع باطری می خواهید؟

---

[75] dukändär

man battri-ye kučik baräye durbin-am mi-xäh-am
I battery small for camera-my want-I
I want small batteries for my camera.

من باطری کوچک برای دوربین ام می خواهم.

bäše. dige či mi-xäh-in
Ok. else what want-you
Ok. What else do you want?

باشه. دیگه چی می خواهین؟

man in čiz-hä rä ham mi-xäh-am
I this things OM also want-I
I also want these items.

من این چیزها را هم می خواهم.

yek **kilo** gušt
one kilo meat

یک کیلو گوشت

nim **kilo** panir
half a kilo cheese

نیم کیلو پنیر

yek **baste** nän[76]

one pack of bread

یک بسته نان

do **tä** xodkär[77]

two pen

دو تا خودکار

yek **ja'be**[78] toxm-e morq[79]

one box of eggs

یک جعبه تخم مرغ

qeymat-e unhä čeqadr mi-šav-ad?

price of they how much is

How much are they?

قیمت آنها چقدر می شود؟

jaman bist hezär toman mi-šavad.

totally twenty thusand Toman becomes.

Altogether it is twenty thusand Toman.

جمعا بیست هزار تومن می شود.

---

[76] näne xošk
[77] qalam
[78] quti
[79] toxom

Grammar hint: Words in bold are called classifiers (Refer to **tä & Classifiers** in the grammar section).

New words		
Persian	**English**	**فارسی**
forušande	shopkeeper	فروشنده
moštari	costumer	مشتری
bin	to see	بین
hame	all	همه
har kodäm	each one	هر کدام
gušt	meat	گوشت
nim	half	نیم
panir	cheese	پنیر
baste	pack	بسته
nän	bread	نان
xodkär	pen	خودکار
ja'be	box, pack	جعبه
toxm-e morq	eggs	تخم مرغ
qeymat	price	قیمت
jaman	altogether	جمعا
hezär	thousand	هزار

Lesson 18   darse hejdah   درس هیجده

Seasons   faslhä   فصل ها
In this lesson, you will learn about different seasons and climates.

dar zemestän havä četor hast?
in winter weather how is
How is the weather in winter?
در زمستان هوا چطور هست؟

dar irän zemestän hamiše sard hast.
in Iran winter always cold is
Winter is always cold in Iran.
در ایران زمستان همیشه سرد هست.

diruz havä dar širäz četor bud?
yesterday weather in Shiraz how was
How was the weather in Shiraz yesterday?
دیروز هوا در شیراز چطور بود؟

diruz havä äftäb-i bud.
yesterday weather sunny was
Yesterday, the weather was sunny.
دیروز هوا آفتابی بود.

alän dar irän fasl-e täbestän hast.
now in Iran season summer is
Now, in Iran it is summer.
الان در ایران فصل تابستان هست.

hamiše zemestän az päyiz[80] sard-tar hast?
always winter from autumn cold-er is
Is winter always colder than autumn?
همیشه زمستان از پاییز سردتر هست؟

bale va päyiz ham **az** täbestän **sard-tar** hast.
yes and autumn also from summer cold-er is
Yes, and autumn is also colder than summer.
بله و پاییز هم از تابستان سردتر هست.

vali täbestän **az** bahär **garm-tar** hast.
but summer from spring hot-er is
But summer is hotter than spring.
ولی تابستان از بهار گرمتر هست.

---

[80] xazän

Grammar hint: Words in bold show the comparative adjective phrases (Refer to **Comparative adjectives** in the grammar section).

New words		
Persian	**English**	**فارسی**
emruz	today	امروز
havä	weather	هوا
abri	cloudy	ابری
bärän	rain	باران
barf	snow	برف
diruz	yesterday	دیروز
bud	was	بود
äftäbi	sunny	آفتابی
fasl	season	فصل
zemestän	winter	زمستان
päyiz	autumn	پاییز
sard	cold	سرد
täbestän	summer	تابستان
bahär	spring	بهار

Lesson 19   darse nuzdah   درس نوزده

| Sigthseeing | jähäye didani | جاهای دیدنی |

In this lesson, you will learn about sightseeing and tourism.

če šahrhäyi dar irän **didan-i** va jäleb hast-and?
what cities in Iran see-able and interesting are-they
What cities in Iran are nice to see and interesting?
چه شهرهایی در ایران دیدنی و جالب هستند؟

bištar-e šahr-hä-ye irän **didan-i** hast-and
most of city –pl-of Iran see-able are-they
Most of cities of Iran are nice to see.
بیشتر شهرهای ایران دیدنی هستند.

esfahän va širäz az šahr-hä-ye bästäni hast-and
Esfahan and Shiraz from city-pl-of ancient are
Esfahan and Shiraz are among ancient cities.
اصفهان و شیراز از شهرهای باستانی هستند.

če jä-hä-yi dar in šahr-hä didani hast-and?
what place-pl in this city-pl see-able are
What places in these cities are for sightseeing?
چه جاهایی در این شهرها دیدنی هستند؟

unhä por az äsär-e bästäni hast-and
they full of monuement-of ancient are-they
They are full of ancient monuements.

آنها پر از آثار باستانی هستند.

jahängard-hä-ye ziyädi az unhä bazdid mi-kon-and
tourist-pl-of a lot from them visit do-they
A lot of tourists visit them.

جهانگردهای زیادی از آنها بازدید می کنند.

albatte šahr-hä-ye digar ham äsär-e qadimi där-and
of course city-pl-of other also monuements of old have
Of course, othr cities have old monuements too.

البته شهرهای دیگر هم آثار قدیمی دارند.

xeyli mamnun. Omidvär-am hame rä be-bin-am
very thanks. Hopefull-am all see-I
Thanks a lot. I hope I will see them all.

خیلی ممنون. امیدوارم همه را ببینم.

Grammar hint: Words like *didani* are formed by adding *i* to the infinitive form of the verb and mean *see-able*. (Refer to **Able suffix** in the grammar section).

New words		
Persian	**English**	**فارسی**
šahr	city	شهر
didan	seeing	دیدن
jäleb	interesting	جالب
bištar	most	بیشتر
bästäni	ancient	باستانی
por	full	پر
äsär	moneuments	آثار
jahängard	tourist	جهانگرد
ziyäd	a lot	زیاد
bazdid kon	to visit	بازدید کن
albatte	of course	البته
digar	other	دیگر
qadimi	old	قدیمی
Omidvär	Hopeful	امیدوار

Lesson 20   darse bist   درس بیست

New Year	**säle jadid**	سال جدید

In this lesson, you will learn about Persian festivals and new year and the related terms.

---

fardä eyd-e noruz hast.
tomorrow feast of Noruz is
Tomorrow is the feast of Noruz.
فردا عید نوروز است.

in eyd dar avvalin ruz-e säl-e no šuru mi-šav-ad
this feast in first day of year of new start become-it
This feast starts at the first day of New Year.
این عید در اولین روز سال نو شروع می شود.

dar eyd, mardom xäne-hä-ye-šun rä tamiz[81] **xähand kard**
in feast, people house-s-their OM clean they will do
In the feast, people will clean their houses.
در عید مردم خانه هایشان را تمیز خواهند کرد.

---

[81] päk käri

unhä lebäs[82]-hä-ye täze **xäh-and xardid** va **xäh-and pušid**
they clothes- of new will-they buy and will-they wear
They will buy and wear new clothes.

آنها لباس های تازه خواهند خرید و خواهند پوشید.

dar eyd, mardom be didan[83]-e hamdigar **xähand raft**.
in feast, people to seeing of each other will go-they
During the feast, people will visit each other.

در عید مردم به دیدن همدیگر خواهند رفت.

in eyd sizdah ruz tul mi-keš-ad.
this feast thirteen day length take-it
This feast lasts for thirteen days.

این عید سیزده روز طول می کشد.

dar ruz-e sizdahom mardom dar birun az xäne qazä mi-xor-and.
in day of thirteen, people in outside of home food eat-they.
On the thirteenth day, people eat outside of their homes.

در روز سیزدهم مردم در بیرون از خانه غذا می خورند.

Grammar hint: The verbs in bold are in future tense (Refer to **Future Tense** in the grammar section).

---

[82] kälä
[83] ziyärat

New words		
Persian	**English**	فارسی
eyd	festivity	عید
noruz	Persian new year's day	نوروز
avvalin	first	اولین
säl	year	سال
no	new	نو
šuru šav	to start	شروع شو
mardom	people	مردم
xäne	house	خانه
tamiz kon	to clean	تمیز کن
lebäs	clothes	لباس
täze	new	تازه
xar	to buy	خر
puš	to wear	پوش
didan	visit	دیدن
hamdigar	each other	همدیگر
sizdah	thirteen	سیزده
tul keš	to last	طول کش
sizdahom	thirteenth	سیزدهم
birun	outside	بیرون
qazä	food	غذا
xor	to eat	خور

Grammar section

This section deals with grammatical items that are important in learning Persian as a second language. This section is not a comprehensive grammar of Persian[84]. These items are chosen by the author based on practical considerations in teaching Persian as a second language and long term experience with the problems that English speakers face in learning Persian. Thus, the numbering of the grammatical items does not show any preference, and it is just for the ease of reference within the book.

The uniqueness of this section is that it is not merely an introduction to the grammatical categories in Persian. It compares the grammatical categories in both English and Persian and explaines about the similarities and differenes between the two languages.

---

[84] For a comprehensive grammar of Persian, refer to Persian grammar that is written by the author and is published by Lincome Europa in Germany.

Adjective:

Adjective is a word or a phrase, which modifies or describes a noun. In English adjectives come before the noun, as in:

new book

good boy

In Persian, unlike in English, the adjective comes after the noun, and the sound '*e*' comes between them, as in:

ketäb-e täze	new book
pesar-e bähuš	smart boy

Adverb:

Adverb is a word, which specifies how, when, or where the action of the verb takes place. For example, in *tonight, John will run there fast*. The words *tonight, there*, and *fast* are adverbs.

In Persian, the equivalent sentence: *emšab, Jän be änjä tond midavad*, the words, *emšab, änjä, tond* are adverbs.

Affix:

Affix is an element, which is added to the beginning or end of a word, and changes or modifies its meaning. At the beginning of a word, it is called prefix and at the end, it is called suffix. For example, in *reassure, re-* is a prefix and in *tasteless, -less* is a suffix. In English, most affixes are for nouns and not for verbs. However, in languages like Persian, there are suffixes and prefixes, which come with the verb. That is, each verb form, takes a different prefix for different tense and a different suffix for different person and numbers. For example, the prefix *mi* comes before a present tense verb, and the suffix *am* comes after the verb for first person singular.

Article:
Article is an element, which indicates whether a noun is definite (specified) or indefinite (unspecified). The definite article in English is *the*, as in *the book* which indicates a specific book. The indefinite article is *a* or *an* as in a book, which indicates *the book* is not specified.

In Persian, the indefinite article is *yek* which comes before the noun, as in *yek mard* 'a man' or *-i*, which come after the noun, as in *mardi* ' a man'. There is no explicit definite article, and when the noun has no indefinite article, it is a definite noun. For example, in *yek mard ämad* 'a man came', the noun is indefinite because of *yek*, but in *mard ämad*, 'The man came' the noun is definite because there is no indefinite article.

Auxiliary verbs:

These are also called helping verbs. They can not come alone in the sentence and they should usually come before the main verb. In English, these verbs are *can, could, shall, should, will, would, may, might*, etc.

In Persian, auxiliary verbs also come before the main verb. They are *bäyad* (should, must), and *šäyad* (may, might), *tavän* (can), and *xäh* (want).

In Persian, unlike in English, the auxiliary verb *tavän* can be in different tenses:
mä xähim tavänest dar emtahän qabul bešavim
we will can in exam admitted be
We will be able to pass the exam.

Helping verbs have no meaning and they are just for grammatical purposes. For example, *will* marks future tense, *have* and *has* mark present perfect, *had* marks past perfect, *do, does* and *did* mark question sentences.

However, we do not need to translate these helping verbs from English into Persian. For example, the words in the brackets are wrong and should be deleted:

I **have** been there.
man (**däram**) unjä bude am

He **has** gone home.
un be xäne (**därad**) rafte

He **had** been there.
un unjä (**däšt**) bude

Do you go home?
šomä (**mikonin**) be xäne miravin

In the above examples, the words in brackets should be deleted that are the literal translation of their equivalent English auxiliary verbs.

Causative verb:
A causative verb describes an action, which someone or something causes someone or something else to do. For example in:

John made George to write the letter.
I had him go to the school.

The verbs *made* and *had* are causative verbs. In English, most causative sentences are formed by using *make* and *have* before the direct object.

In Persian, like in English, there are causative verbs, which come before the main verb, as in:

Ali bä'es šod man be xäne beravam
Ali cause became I to home go-I
Ali made me to go home.

There is also a causative suffix, *-än* which can be added to the main verb to change it to a causative verb. For example, the verb *xor* in:

Ali sib rä xord
Ali apple OM ate
Ali ate the apple.

becomes a causative verb in:

Ahmad sib rä be Ali xor-än-d
Ahmad apple OM to Ali eat-causative-past
Ahmad made Ali to eat the apple

Classifiers:

In Persian, a noun does not take a plural form when it comes after a number (yek, do, etc.) or a classifier (čand, meqdäri, xeyli, etc.), as in:

yek ketäb	one book
do tä ketab	two books
čand tä ketäb	some books
xeyli ketäb	many books

Colloquial forms:

In Persian, words in the spoken form are usually shorter than in the written form. Here are some examples of the differences between written and spoken forms of words.

Written form	Spoken form	Meaning
ast	e	is
bekon	kon	do
dän	dun	know
nešin	šin	sit
kodäm	kodum	which
arzän	arzun	cheap
gerän	gerun	expensive
sobhäne	sobhune	breakfast
äsän	äsun	easy
tamäm	tamum	finished
mišavad	miše	becomes
rä	ro/o	OM
mi-dah-am	mi-d-am	I give
mi-rav-am	mi-r-am	I go

mi-xäh-am	mi-x-äm	I want
mi-guy-am	mi-g-am	I say
mi-tavän-am	mi-tun-am	I can
mi-äy-am	mi-yäm	I come
mi-kon-ad	mi-kon-e	I do
mi-šav-am	mi-š-am	I become
mi-dah-ad	mi-d-e	he gives

Comparative adjectives:

For comparative adjectives, in English we add 'more' at the beginning or 'er' at the end of the adjective, as in:

new   newer

intelligent   more intelligent

In Persian, a comparative adjective is formed by adding 'tar' to the end, as in:

täze   täze-tar   newer

bä huš   bähuš-tar   more intelligent

In English, to make a superlative adjective, we add 'most' at the beginning or 'est' at the end of the adjective, as in:

new   newest

intelligent most intelligent

In Persian, the superlative adjective is formed by adding 'tarin' to the end, as in:

täze	täze-tarin	newest
bä huš	bähuš-tarin	most intelligent

Complementiser:

In English the words like *when, who, whose* can be used for two different purposes:

1. as a question word, as in:
When did you go?
Who came?

2. as a complementiser. That is, they connect a complement sentence to the main sentence, as in:
I went home when you came to the school.
The man who is the chief came here.

In Persian the question and complementiser forms of these words are different, and unlike in English, we can not use one for the other. For example:
key: when
ki: who

are question words, but:

vaqtike: when

ike: who

are complementiser words. We can see the difference in the following examples:

un key   raft
he when   went
'When did he go?'

ki ämad
who came
'Who came?'

man be xäne raft-am vaqtike   to be madrese ämad-i
I   to home went-I   when you to school came-I
'I went home when you came to the school.'

mard ike   ra'is ast be injä ämad
man who   chief is   to here came
'The man who is the chief came here.'

In Persian, unlike in English, we can pluralise the question words, as in:

ki   who   kiyä   who (plural)

Compound verbs:
There are few verbs in Persian which are simple one-word verbs. A large number of verbs in Persian are compound. That is, they are formed with a noun or an adjective followed by a simple verb form. The verb gets different person and number ending and the noun or adjective stays the same. The most common compound verbs are:

Compound verbs that are made by kon 'do'

'ebädat mikonam	I worship
avaz mikonam	I change
bäz mikonam	I open
bäzi mikonam	I play
da'vä mikonam	I fight
do'ä mikonam	I pray
donbäl mikonam	I follow
edäre mikonam	I manage
ehsäs mikonam	I feel

ejäre mikonam	I rent
entexäb mikonam	I choose
ešare mikonam	I point
eštebäh mikonam	I make a mistake
estefräq mikonam	I vomit
esterähat mikonam	I relax
exräj mikonam	I sack
ezdeväj mikonam	I marry
farämuš mikonam	I forget
garm mikonam	I heat
haml mikonam	I carry
hesäb mikonam	I calculate
jelogiri mikonam	I prevent
kansel mikonam	I cancel
kär mikonam	I work
kär mikonam	I work
kasb mikonam	I acquire, obtain
keräye mikonam	I rent

komak mikonam	I help
lams mikonam	I touch
masraf mikonam	I use, consume
masxare mikonam	I ridicule
maxlut mikonam	I mix
mo'ämele mikonam	I deal with
mohäjerat mikonam	I migrate
moläqät mikonam	I meet
mosähebe mikonam	I interview
negäh mikonam	I look
pahn mikonam	I spread
päk mikonam	I clean
pärk mikonam	I park
pasandäz mikonam	I save
paxš mikonam	I distribute
peydä mikonam	I find
por mikonam	I fill
post mikonam	I post

qabul mikonam	I accept
qarz mikonam	I borrow
qat mikonam	I cut
qofl mikonam	I lock
rang mikonam	I colour
residegi mikonam	I investigate
rezerv mikonam	I reserve
šäne mikonam	I comb
sargarm mikonam	I entertain
šekäyat mikonam	I complain
šoru' mikonam	I start
šuxi mikonam	I joke
ta'yid mikonam	I confirm
tafrih mikonam	I enjoy, amuse
tajrobe mikonam	I experience
tamam mikonam	I finish
tark mikonam	I leave
tazriq mikonam	I inject

tekrär mikonam	I repeat
vahšat mikonam	I get scared
xaräb mikonam	I destroy
xarj mikonam	I spend
xoddäri mikonam	I refuse
xošk mikonam	I dry
za'f mikonam	I faint

Compound verbs that are made by deh 'give'

ejäze midaham	I let
este'fä midaham	I resign
extär midaham	I warn
javab midaham	I answer
nejät midaham	I save
nešän midaham	I show
pul midaham	I pay
qarz midaham	I lend
qurt midaham	I swallow
ra'y midaham	I vote

rešve midaham	I bribe
tahvil midaham	I submit
taqyir midaham	I change
tarjih midaham	I prefer
tašxis midaham	I recognize
tozih midaham	I explain
xabar midaham	I notify

Compound verbs that are made by zan 'hit'

dast mizanam	I touch, I clap
hads mizanam	I guess
zang mizanam	I ring

Compound verbs that are made by šo 'become'

del tang mišavam	I miss
dur mišavam	I get away
närähat mišavam	I get upset
nazdik mišavam	I come close
qabul mišavam	I pass

qarq mišavam	I drown
rad mišavam	I fail
savär mišavam	I ride
xafe mišavam	I suffocate
xaste mišavam	I get tired

To make a sentence with these compound verbs, you should put the tense suffix on the simple verb which is the second part, and not on the first part, as in:

man asb savär mi šav am

I horse ride become-I

I ride the horse.

But you can not say:

*man asb   mi   savär   am

Unusual compound verbs:

Most of Persian verbs are compound. Some compound verbs have unusual meaning and look like an idiom. Some examples are:

be kär bor
to take to work
to use

sarmä xor
to eat cold
to catch a cold

dir kon
to do late
to be late

donbäl gard
to wonder behind.
to look for

ajale där
to have a hurry
to be in a hurry

piyäde šav
to become on foot
to get off

savär šov
to become on board
to get on

vaqt kon
to do time
to have time

be hamräh ävar
to accompany bring
to bring with oneself

be ta'xir oft
to delay fall
to delay

bar ohde där
to responsibility have
to be responsible

be nazar ras
to look reach
to look like

az dast dah
to give from hand
to lose

az sar gir
to pick from head
to restart

be sar bar
to take to head
to live

surat gir
to get face
to happen

bar pä šav
to become on foot
to be held

šomorde šav
to become counted
to be taken into account

päyän dah
to give an end
to finish

yäd kon
to do memory
to remember

be dast gir
to get to hand
to take over

tartibe asar dah
to give trace order
to take into account

be hesäb ävar
to bring to account
to count

be donbäl där
to have to behind
to result in

be zabän ävar
to bring to tongue
to utter

Conjunctions:

Beside simple conjunctions like *va* (and), different types of compound conjunctions are used in Persian. Some are as in below:

ham…ham…   both …and…
ham Ali raft ham Hasan.   Both Ali and Hasan went.

če…….če……   whether…..or…
če Ali beravad če Hasan, man na-xäh-am raft
Whether Ali goes or Hasan, I won't go.

Copula (to be):

Copula is a verb which links the subject to the predicate (which is a noun or an adjective). English copula verbs are *be, become* and *appear*. The verb *be* (which has different forms: *be, am, is, are, was, were*) is the most frequent copula used in English:

| John | is | a student. |
| subject | copula | predicate |

| The cat | is | hungry. |
| subject | copula | predicate |

In Persian, the copula verb is *hast* which has different forms for different persons and numbers:

I am	hast-am
You are	hast-i
He is	hast
We are	hast-im
You(PL) are	hast-in
They are	hast-and

Thus, in a sentence, first, there is a noun or an adjective and then a *to be* verb:

man	dänešju	hast am
subject	predicate	copula

I am a student.

to	gorosne	hasti
subject	predicate	copula

You are hungry.

The verb *to be* in English can be an auxiliary verb, as in :
I am going home.
or it can be a main verb, as in:
I am at home.

In Persian, *to be* verb is always a main verb, as in here:

man xub   (hast) am

I   good   am

I am fine.

The verb *hast* takes personal suffixes, as in here:

(hast) am   I am
(hast) I   you are
(hast)   he/she/it is
(hast) im   we are
(hast) in   you are
(hast) and   they are

hast can be deleted in conversation. Thus, the above sentence can be :*man xab am.*

Difficult English words for Persian speakers:
Since in Persian there are no *w* and *th*, and no consonant clusters starting with *s*, the words containing these sounds are difficult and their pronunciation is usually not correct. The following passage is an example of such a challenge in pronunciation for Persian speakers:

Therefore, the story stipulated by the stupid students was this: wonderfully wealthy women went after the thief, while we waited with Theodore. He was stunned because the thief had acquired monies equivalent to three weeks work.

It would be pronounced by Persian speakers as:
Derefore, de estory estipulated by de estudents vas dis: vonderfully vealthy voman vent after de tief, vhile ve vaited vith Teodore. He vas estunned because de tief had acquired monies equivalent to tree veeks vork.

Double negative:
In English, except for few dialects, there is no double negative in making negative sentences. For example, in the sentence, *I saw nothing*, it is *nothing* which is negative and the verb is in the positive form. However, in some dialects like Black English, it is said: *I did not see nothing*. This called double negative because both the verb *did not see* and the adverb *nothing* are negative.

In Persian, there is always a double negative with an adverb. Thus, for the same sentence, in Persian both *nothing* and *see* are negative:

man   hič čiz   na   didam
I   nothing   not see I
I saw nothing.

English words with no equivalent in Persian:
Some English words have no equivalents in Persian. These words are usually explained with a phrase or a sentence in Persian. Some examples are:
hang over
home sick
nostalgia
sea sick
sleep over
that's it
to care

English words with different Persian meaning:
Some English words have two or more different meanings in Persian. Thus, to learn where to use each word is a challenge for Persian students. Some examples are:

know	dän (for knowledge)	šenäs (for recognition)
funny	šux (a funny person)	xande där (a funny thing)
sure	hatman (certainly)	motma'en (confident)

Ok	bäše (Ok!)	xob	(fine, good)
free	äzäd (released)	majjäni	(free of charge)
student	däneš ämuz (school)	dänešju (tertiary)	
busy	šoluq (crowded)	mašqul (busy with)	
then	pas (so, therefore)	ba'd	(after)
fat	čäq (obese)	čarbi	(fat in food)
half	nim (time, weight, length)	nesf (things)	
new	täze (physical inanimate)	qadimi (non physical)	
old	pir (animate)	kohne (inanimate)	

Future Tense:

In English, the future tense is formed by adding an auxiliary verb like *will* or *shall*, or *going to* before the main verb, as in *we will go* or *we are going to go*.

In Persian, the future tense in the spoken style is the same as in the present tense. Thus, we can use present tense form to talk about future. For example:

man   fardä   mi-rav-am
I   tomorrow   go
'I will go tomorrow.'

Adverbs of time like *fardä* (tomorrow) differentiate between future, simple present and continuous present forms:

man alän mi-rav-am
I now go
'I am going.'

man har ruz mi-rav-am
I every day go
'I go every day.'

In the formal style, the future tense is formed by adding the verb *xäh* (want) before the main verb. *xäh* gets the personal ending but the main verb always stays in the past tense form, as in:

xäh-am raft	I will go
xäh-i raft	You will go
xäh-ad raft	He will go
xäh-im raft	We will go
xäh-id raft	You (Pl) will go
xäh-and raft	They will go

In these examples, the verb *xäh* takes different endings for different persons, and the verb *raft* which is the past tense of *rav* 'go' always stays the same.

Greetings in Persian:

To learn the way people greet in a language is not just learning the words and phrases. It is related with the culture of the speakers of that language. Thus, to greet properly in the language, one should become familiar with the culture. For example, in Persian, using a singular second person pronoun to call strangers or people higher than the speaker in age or position is impolite and sometimes is regarded as an insult. Therefore, except for close friends and children, we should always use the plural form. The language learner won't know the difference unless the cultural implication of addressing people is also known.

In Persian like many other languages, greetings are mostly expressed as one or two word phrases, and these phrases usually do not have a subject. They usually consist of a noun and an adjective. The order in which the words in these phrases come is different from English. For example, in:

sobh   *bexeyr*
morning   good
'good morning'

The noun *sobh* comes before *bexyer*, while in English; it is first the adjective *good* and then the noun *morning*.

Since Persian is one of the languages which is rich in formalities and pleasantries, it has many politeness phrases and idioms which are used depending on the situation, the people involved, and so on.

Idioms:

As with any other language, Persian has many idioms that can not be literally translated into English, and the meaning of phrase should be learned as a whole. Some examples are:

manzur et chi hast?
your intention what is
What do you mean?

ma'ni yeš chi hast?
its meaning what is
What does it mean?

rästeš
its truth
actually

be jäye
in place of
instead of

zahmat kišidin
you pulled the trouble
you got into trouble.

ma'zerat mixäm
I want pardon
I apologize

delam baraye šomä tang ode
my heart has become tight for you
I have missed you.

čerä ke na
why that no
why not

ki be kiye
who is whom
who cares!

dastetun dard nakone
you hands may not hurt
God bless you.

xaste nabäšin
tired not-be-you
You may not be tired.

age man jäye šomä budam
if I was in your place
if I were you

taklif rošan kardan
to turn on the task

to clarify the situation

delam mixähad
my hearts want
I like

az jomle
from all
including

qäbele šomä rä nadäre
it does not have your value
it is nothing for you.

jätun xäli bud
you place was empty
you missed it.

Imperatives:

An imperative sentence is formed to order someone to do something or to make a request from someone, or to give directions. An imperative verb addresses only the second person, both singular and plural. In English, the imperative verb is the base verb like, *go, come, read*, etc. as in:

Go home!

Please come here!

In Persian, the imperative verb is also formed using the base verb, like *xän* 'read' by adding the prefix *be* to the beginning of the verb, as in: **be-xän** 'read!'. In Persian, imperatives have two forms for the second person singular and plural, as in:

be-xän   'read!'   (asking just one person to read)
be-xän-in 'read!'   (asking two or more people to read)

Infinitive:

Infinitive is a basic form of the verb which usually appears in the dictionary. For example, English verbs are all in infinitive forms in the dictionary like, *to go, to come, to study*, etc. If we drop it from the beginning of the verb, the verb will be in the imperative (order) form, as in *go!, come!, study!*.

In Persian, the infinitive marker is *an* which comes at the end of the verb, as in *raft-an* 'to go', *ämad-an* 'to come', and *xänd-an* 'to study.

In Persian, when we drop the infinitive *an*, the verb stays in the past tense form. So, in ordinary dictionaries, the verb form is in infinitive form and it is difficult for a non native speaker to make a present tense, a future tense, or an imperative verb form out of it. That is why; in this book we introduce verbs in their imperative forms and make other forms from it. For example the verb *to go* is *rav*, which is the imperative form. We can add suffixes and prefixes to this form to make present, future, etc.

To understand the difference between the infinitive, past and present forms of Persian verbs, see the following list:

Present tense		past tense	Infiniti
xor	eat	xord	xordan
xäb	sleep	xäbid	xäbidan
rav	go	raft	raftan
äy	come	ämad	ämadan
nešin	sit	nešast	nešastan
bin	see	did	didan
guy	say	goft	goftan

Intransitive verbs:

In Persian, a simple sentence can be just a single verb! Because of the inflection, the subject ending is already on the verb, and there is no need for the subject, and it can be deleted. While in English, you can not make a sentence without a subject. Consider these sentences.

(man) mi xäb am

I am sleeping.

(man) mi dav am

I am running.

As we see, these two sentences are just two verbs. The subject marker is *am* at the end of verb. It shows that the subject is 'I'.

That is why, it is so important to use the endings for different persons:

(man) mi dav am
I am running.

(to) mi dav i
You are running.

(un) mi dav ad
He is running.

(mä) mi dav im
We are running.

(šomä) mi dav id
You are running.

(unhä) mi dav and
They are running.

Therefore, as you see, we can make a sentence in Persian just by using a verb. That is, we take the root verb *dav*, and add the present tense prefix *mi* and the ending for subject *am*. These types of sentences, which have no object, are called 'intransitive sentences'.

Interrogatives (Questions):

There are different types of questions in every language. In English, the most common types are Yes-No questions and WH questions. A Yes-No question usually is formed by using *do, does*, and *did* in the beginning of the sentence, as in:
Did he come yesterday?

In Persian, Yes-No questions are only formed by a rise in intonation at the end of the sentence. Thus, unlike in English, there is no change in word order, as in:
šomä   sib mixorid
šomä   sib mixorid?↑

In the written style, the word *äyä* is added to the start of the sentence but in the spoken style it is not used.
The plane is leaving?   äyä haväpeymä harekat mikonad?
The plane is leaving.   haväpeymä harekat mikonad.
(lit: plane move do-it)
Is the plane leaving?   haväpeymä harekat mikonad?

In English, this type of questioning (rising intonation) is used in conversation, as in:
The plane is leaving? ↑

WH questions in English are formed by using a question word *like who, where, what, why, which, when*, etc. in the beginning of the sentence, and the category being questioned (subject, or object) is deleted. The sentence also needs a helping verb like *do*, *does*, and *did*, as in:
Where did he go?

In Persian, making a WH question is easier than in English. There is no need to use a helping verb and changing the tense of the verb. The question word is usually comes in the place of the missing subject or object. The question words in Persian are: *kojä* (where), *čerä* (why), *key* (when), *če* (what), *četor* (how), *ki* (who), *kodäm* (which). See these examples:
bänk kojä   hast?
bank where is
Where is the bank?

čerä muze baste ast?
why museum closed is
Why is the museum closed?

jašn key šuru' mišavad?
festival when start become-it
When does the festival begin?

un če miguyad?
he what say-he
What is he saying?

četor änjä beravam?
how there go-I
How do I go there?

un ki hast?
she who is
Who is she?

kodäm behtar ast?
which better is
Which one is the best?

keš:

The verb *keš* is used in those compound verbs, which denote some continuity and extension of the act like: *sigär keš, naqqäši keš, deräz keš, tul keš.*

Verbs plus prepositions:

In Persian some verbs are followed by specific prepositions. Some examples are:

baräye	deltang šodan bräye
dar	dexälat kardan dar
bä	tasädof kardan bä
	ruberu šodan bä
	jang kardan bä
	harf zadan bä
	sohbat kardan bä
be	telefon kardan be
	tosiye kardan be
	asar gozäštan be
	javäb dädan be
	rasidan be

	hamle karan be
	aqide dästan be
	rešve dädan be
	dars dädan be
	komak kardan be
	telefon zadan be
	lagad zadan be
	guš kardan be
	ehtiyäj dästan be
	ta'ärof kardan be
	dastur dädan be
	eqdäm kardan be
	niyäz dästan be
	ehteräm kardan be
	fohš dädan be
	e'temäd kardan be
az	tašakor kardan az
	porsidan az
	ozr xästan az
	xästan az
	ejtenäb kardan az
	moväzebat kardan az

	bälä raftan az
	šekäyat kardan az
	enteqäd kardan az
	gozaštan az
	defä kardan az
	mahrum kardan az
	bäzdid kardan az
	peyravi kardan az
	hemäyat kardan az
	emtenä' kardan az
	darxäst kardan az
	este'fä dädan az
	aqab nešini kardan az
	aks gereftan az
	estefäde kardan az

Negatives:

In English, a negative verb is formed by adding *not* after the auxiliary *do, does* or *did*, as in:

I do not eat.

He does not eat.
You did not eat.

In Persian, to make a negative verb, the prefix *na* is placed before the verb, as in:

un be tehrän raft

(lit: he to Tehran went-he)

He went to Tehran.

un be tehrän na-raft

He did not go to Tehran.

For the future tense, *na* is added to the first verb, as in:

un be tehrän xähad raft

he to Tehran want-he went

He will go to Tehran.

un be tehrän na-xähad raft

he to Tehran no-want-he went

He will not go to Tehran.

The negative form of the *to be* verb *hast* is *nist*, as in:

Ali tešne hast
Ali thirsty is
Ali is thirsty.

Ali tešne nist
Ali thirsty not is
Ali is not thirsty.

Thus, in the negative form, *nist* replaces *hast*.

Noun:

Nouns are words, which denote a person, e.g. *John*, an animal, e.g. *cat* or a thing, e.g. *table*, or a concept, e.g. *wish*. Nouns can be a subject or object in the sentence. Thus, in the sentence like *the cat eats the meat*, *cat* is a noun and at the same time the subject of the sentence and *meat* is also a noun and at the same time the object of the sentence. Nouns can be singular or plural. The way we make a plural noun is different among languages.

In English to make a noun plural, we put *'(e)s'* at the end of the noun as in:

book   books
glass   glasses

In Persian, we should put *hä* at the end, as in:

book   ketäb
books   ketäb hä

There are some other markers for plurality which are borrowed from Arabic like *än, in, ät,* in *deraxtän* 'trees', *mo'allemän* 'teachers', *bäqät* 'gardens'.

In English, there are some nouns, which have irregular plurals, as in:
fish   fish
tooth   teeth

In Persian, there are also a few irregular plurals, which are borrowed from Arabic, as in:
eyd 'festivity'   *a'yäd* 'festivities'
täjer 'businessman'   *tojjär* 'businesspersons'

Object:

An object is a noun or a pronoun which is linked to the subject and the verb. As mentioned in English, the object comes after the verb, as in:

John came home.

S   V   O

In Persian, the object comes after the subject and before the verb, as in:

Ali   yek sib xord

S   O   V

Ali   one apple ate

Ali ate an apple.

An object can be direct or indirect. In English, the direct object has no preposition, as in:

I   saw   John.

S   V   DO

An indirect object usually takes a preposition, as in:

He   is going   to school.

S   V   IO

In Persian, when a preposition like: *bä* (with), *be* (to), *dar* (in, at, on), *az* (from) *baräye* (for) comes before the object, it is an indirect objects in:

Ali   az madrase   ämad

S   IO   V

Ali from school came
Ali came from the school.

man	bä mäšin	be xäne	miravam
S	IO	IO	V
I	with car	to home	go-I

I go home by car.

šomä	dar otäq	bemänin
S	IO	V
you	in room	stay-you

You stay in the room.

man	baräye Ali	näme	nevestam
S	IO	DO	V
I	for Ali	letter	wrote-I

I wrote a letter to Ali.

If the object has no preposition, it is a direct object:

man	sib rä	xordam
S	DO	V
I	apple-OM	ate-I

I ate the apple.

Ali   un mard rä   did

S	DO	V
Ali	that man OM	saw

Ali saw that man.

šomä	mašin rä	bebarin
S	DO	V
you	car OM	take-you

You take the car!

Object marker rä:

This is an important suffix which comes after the direct object in the sentence. However, there are exceptions to this and that is why, it is confusing for non-native speakers when to use it. As a general rule, it comes after the direct object, as in:

man	sib rä	mi-xor-am
I	apple	eat-1SG

I am eating the apple.

It is also used as:

(a) when the object is plural, as in:

man	ketäb -hä -rä	mi-xän-am
I	book -PL -OM	read-1SG

I am reading the books.

(b) when the object is followed by a possessive suffix, as in:

man   ketäb -am -rä mi-xän-am
I   book -my –OM read-1SG

I am reading my book.

(c) when the object is preceded by a demonstrator like in (this) or un (that), as in:

man   in   ketäb -rä   mi-xän-am
I   this   book -OM   read-1SG

I am reading this book.

Passive voice:

In a passive sentence, there is an object and a verb but no subject. In English a passive is usually made of a to be verb followed by the past participle of the verb, as in:

I ate an apple.

The apple **was eaten**.

In Persian, the passive verb is made of the past tense of verb plus *e* followed by the past tense of *šav* (become), as in:

man sib xord-am

sib **xord-e šod**

Past Tense:

In English, the past tense is formed either by adding (e)d to the present tense form of the verb, as in *watch, watch-ed*, or its form is completely different from the present tense form, as in *go, went*.

In Persian, some verbs are also regular and take *-d* ending to form a past tense (as in *xor* 'eat', *xor-d*). However, like English most verbs are irregular (as in *paz* 'cook', *poxt*). Thus, to make past tense sentences, you need to learn the past tense forms of most verbs. The personal suffixes are added to the past tense form of verbs, as in these examples:

I am eating	man mi-xor-am
I ate	man xor-d-am
You are eating	to mi-xor-i
You ate	to xor-d-i
S/he is eating	un mi-xor-ad
S/he ate	un xor-d

For the third person singular (he, she, it), there is no personal suffix in the past tense. The present and past tense form of most common simple verbs in Persian are as follows:

Present tense		Past tense	
ävar	bring	ävard	brought
äviz	hang	ävixt	hung
äy	come	ämad	came
band	close	bast	closed
bär	rain	bärid	rained
bar	take	bord	took
bargard	return	bargašt	returned
bin	see	did	saw
bor	cut	borid	cut
čarx	turn	čarxid	turned
čin	pick	čid	picked
dah	give	däd	gave
dän	know	dänest	knew
där	have	däšt	had
dav	run	david	ran
duz	saw	duxt	sew
furuš	sell	furuxt	sold

guy	say	goft	said
hast	is	bud	was, were
ist	stop	istäd	stopped
kan	dig	kand	dug
kär	plant	käšt	planted
kon	do	kard	did
koš	kill	košt	killed
mäl	rub	mälid	rubbed
män	stay	mänd	stayed
mir	die	mord	died
nešin	sit	nešast	sat
par	fly	parid	flew
päš	sprinkle	päšid	sprinkled
paz	cook	poxt	cooked
raqs	dance	raqsid	danced
ras	reach	rasid	reached
rav	go	raft	went
riz	pour	rixt	poured

šav	become	šod	became
säz	make	säxt	made
šenäs	know(some one)	šenäxt	knew
šur	wash	šost	washed
suz	burn	suxt	burned
tavän	can	tavänest	could
xäb	sleep	xäbid	slept
xäh	want	xäst	wanted
xän	read	xänd	read
xar	buy	xarid	bought
xaz	crawl	xazid	crawled
xor	eat	xord	ate
zan	hit	zad	hit

Persian words with similar pronunciation:

There are some words in Persian which are mistaken for each other by the language learners, as thir pronunciation are close to each other. Some examples are:

vos'at	extension, size
vasat	middle
mašqul	busy
moškel	hard, problem
darmän	treatment
darämad	income
mahall	place
mahalle	suburb
xarj	expense
xärej	outside
zamin	ground, floor, earth
zamän	time, era

xäh	want, ask
xar	buy, donkey
xor	eat
par	feather, jump
por	full
pir	old
bar	take
bär	load, rain
bor	cut
bur	blonde
kešti	ship
košti	wrestling
säz	build, make
suz	burn

amu	uncle
mu	hair
hamle	attack
hämele	pregnant
haml	carrying
bäd	wind
ba'd	later, next
bad	bad
tärix	history, date
tärik	dark
šahr	city
še'r	poem
šir	lion, tap, milk

äsän	easy
arzän	cheap

dar	door, in
där	have
dur	far
dir	late

qäbel	able
qabl	before
qabul	acceptance

älat	equipment
ellat	reason

mosähebe	interview
mohäsebe	calculation

movaffaq	successful
moväfeq	agreed
ajib	strange
jäleb	interesting
marbut	related
martub	wet
jadid	new
šadid	strong
kun	ass
xun	blood
tavassot	by
vasat	middle

paridan	to jump, to fly (a bird)
parväz kardan	to fly

qabl az	before (preposition)
qablan	before (adverb)
qabli	the previous one

xayyät	tailor
xäyat	your testicle

qahve	coffee
qahbe	prostitute

guy	to say
gäy	to fuck

Persian words with different meanings:

As with English, there are many words in Persian with different meanings. The commonly used ones that are mistaken by the language learners are as follow:

dah	give	ten
emtehän	trial	test
goftan	to say	to tell
mašqul	busy with	engaged (phone)

142

räst	straight	true	right
sir	garlic	full (of eating)	
šir	milk	tap	lion
šoluq	naughty	crowded	
šur	wash	salty	
tä	until	for (reason)	
xaräb	rotten	demolished	out of order

Person and number:

These terms are used to differentiate among pronouns. English has first person singular, e.g. *I*, and plural, e.g. *we*, and second person singular, e.g. *you*, and plural, e.g. *you*, and third person singular, e.g. *he, she, it*, and plural, e.g. *they*.

In Persian, there are also first person singular, e.g. *man*, first person plural e.g. *mä*, second person singular, e.g. *to*, second person plural, e.g. *šomä* and third person singular, e.g. *un*, and third person plural, e.g. *unhä*.

Therefore, in Persian, unlike in English, there are two different pronouns for the second person: *to* (singular), and *šomä* (plural). On the other hand, in English, there are three different forms of the third person singular (*he, she, it*) while in Persian it is just one form (*un*).

Number refers to the singularity or plurality of a word. In English, a word is either singular like *book*, or plural like *books*. The plurality in English is usually shown by adding *(e)s* to the end of the word.

In Persian, a word is also either singular as in *ketäb* (book) or plural as in *ketäb-hä*. The plurality in Persian is usually shown by adding *hä* at the end of the word.

Politeness:
Persian is one of those languages, which are rich in polite words and phrases to show politeness and formalities. As it is expected, the literal translation of these words and phrases is different from their original meaning. That is, almost all of them are idiomatic and it is difficult to translate them literally into English. That is why learning polite forms are always a difficult part of the language for the language learners.

To learn these phrases, we should go back to the context in which they are used and try to relate the meaning to the context. However, sometimes the same phrase has different usages in different contexts of politeness. Thus, the learner should be able to guess the relevant meaning based on the specific context. For example, one of these phrases is: ***befarmäyin***. This phrase has so many different politeness denotations based on different contexts. Some of them are as follows:

How can I help you?
Context: when you enter a shop and say hello and the shopkeeper says: befarmäyin.

Come in
Context: when you knock the door and the person inside says befarmäyin.

Here you are
Context: when you are going to pay the money for your shopping in the shop, you the money to him and you say befarmäyin.

Please go on, continue
Context: when you are talking and someone interrupts, and then the listener tells you befarmäyin.

Take a seat

Context: when you enter somewhere and the guy inside offers you a seat and says befarmäyin.

You go first

Context: when you are entering somewhere with someone else, you say to him befarmäyin.

There are many other polite phrases, which are not easily translated into English and should be considered within the context. There is no one-by-one equivalence for these phrases in English. Thus, they should only be learned in the context by introducing the cultural implication of the phrase. For example, to learn the phrase *'dastetun dard nakonad'*, you should know that in this culture, anything you do for someone should be verbally rewarded with this phrase.

Possession:

A possession relation is between two nouns like 'the girl's shoes', 'the leg of the table'. In the example 'the girl's shoes', the word 'girl' is called 'possessor' and the word 'shoes' is called 'possessed'. That means: 'the girl' possesses 'the shoes'. That is, possession is between two nouns where one is the owner (possessor) and the other one is the owned (possessed). For example, in *John's book, John* is the owner (possessor) of the book and *book* is the owned (possessed) noun. In English, there are two different forms of this possession: when there is an animate possessor, like *John, boy, animal, cat*, etc., it comes before the possessed word and there is a *'s* between them, like in: *John's money, kid's toy,* and *student's book*. When the possessor is inanimate, like *'table', 'house'* and *'tea'*, it comes after the possessed word and there is an *of* between them, like in: *'the leg of the table', 'the roof of the house', 'a cup of tea'*.

In English, there are possessive pronouns which come before the noun and specify whether it belong to the first, second or thirds person. See these examples:

my book	our book
your book	your book
her/his book	their book

In Persian, the possession with pronouns is the same as in English, but possessive pronouns come after the verb as in:

ketäb-am	ketäb-emun
ketäb-et	ketäb-etun
ketäb-eš	ketäb-ešun

In the possessive relation between two nouns, the possessed always comes before the possessor and we insert -e (which is called Ezäfe) after the possessed and before the possessor, as in:

kKafš   e   doxtar
shoes   POSS   girl
the girl's shoes

ketäb   e   Ali
book   POSS   Ali
Ali's book

saqf   e   xäne
roof   POSS   house
the roof of the house

päye   e   miz
leg   POSS   table
the leg of the table

Where there are more than two words in the possession relation, we should start from the last one to translate it in Persian. For example, in 'my son's book', the order is opposite to English. It means that in Persian 'book' then 'son' and then 'my' as in:

ketäb　e　　pesar　e　　man
book　POSS　son　POSS　my
my son's book

'Ezafe' takes the form of *ye* when the noun ends in a vowel.
leg of table　　　　päye ye miz
As we see, in Persian there is no difference in the order when the possessor is animate or inanimate.

Prefix be-:
This prefix comes before the verb and its usage is different in different situations. Look at these sentences:
man šäyad **be**-ravam
I　　may　　go-I
I may go.

man bäyad **be**-ravam
I　　should　　go-I
I should go.

man mixäham be unjä **be**-ravam
I   want-I   to there go-I
I wanted to go there.

man dust däram be unjä **be**-ravam
I   like have-I to there go-I
I like to go there

šomä **be**-rav-in
you   go-you
You go!

As you see, these verbs take '*be*' in the beginning instead of '*mi*'. This prefix is called subjunctive. Thus:

1   when the sentence has an auxiliary word like *bäyad* 'should', and *šäyad* 'may', the verb comes with 'be':
man be xäne **mi**-ravam
I   to   home   go-I
I am going home.

man bäyad be xäne **be**-ravam
I should to home go-I
I should go home.

man šäyad be xäne **be**-ravam
I may to home go-I
I may go home.

2   When the verb is an order (imperative) verb, it takes 'be:

šomä be xäne **mi**-rav-in
you to home go-you
You are going home.

šomä be xäne **be**-rav-in
you to home go-you
You go home!

3   When there are two verbs in the sentence, the second verb takes 'be':

man mixäham be xäne **be**-ravam
I want-I to home go-I
I want to go home.

man dust däram be xäne **be**-ravam
I   like have-I to home go-I
I like to go home.

man <u>mitavänam</u> be xäne **be**-<u>ravam</u>
I   can-I   to home go-I
I can go home.

Preposition:
Preposition is a word, which comes before the object in the sentence, and by itself, has no meaning. As mentioned before, the common prepositions in English and their Persian equivalents are **in, at, on** (*dar*), **to** (*be*), **from** (*az*), and **with** (*bä*).

Present perfect tense:
In English the present perfect tense is formed by *have* (*has* for the third person singular) and the third form of the verb which is called past participle. For example, in *I have gone there*, the verb is in present perfect tense (*have* plus the third form of *go*, which is *gone*).

In Persian, the present perfect tense is formed by the past tense form of the verb plus the suffix *e* plus the verb endings. For example, *I have gone* would be *man raft-e-am* (the past tense form of *rav* '**go**' + *e*+ *am*).

Present tense:

The present tense in English has two forms:
Present simple, as in: *John is going home now.*
Present continous, as in: *John goes home every day.*
As we see, in the simple present tense, *to be* (*am, is, are,* etc.) comes before the verb and the verb takes *-ing*. In the continuous present tense, the verb is in its base form and takes *(e)s* for the third person singular.

In Persian, it is easy to form a present tense, because both simple and continuous forms are expressed with the same form. To form a present tense sentence, we take the base verb (which is always in the imperative form) and add *mi* before it. Then, we add the personal suffixes *-am, -i, -ad, -im, -id, -and* to the end of the verb, as in these examples:

man	ketäb	mi-xän-am	I read the book.
to	ketäb	mi-xän-i	You read the book.
un	ketäb	mi-xän-ad	S/he reads the book.
mä	ketäb	mi-xän-im	We read the book.

| šomä | ketäb | mi-xän-in | You read the book. |
| unhä | ketäb | mi-xän-and | They read the book. |

To differentiate between simple and continuous forms, we use time adverbs. For example, in:

Ali   alän   be xäne   mi-rav-ad
Ali   now   to home   go-he
Ali is going home now.

We know the sentence is simple present because of the adverb *alän* 'now'.

On the other hand, the sentence in below is continuous present because of the adverb *har ruz* 'every day':

Ali   har ruz   be xäne   mi-rav-ad
Ali   every day   to home   go-he
Ali goes home every day.

The verb *där* 'to have' does not take *mi* in the present tense:
man ketäb däram
I   book   have-I
I have a book.

As we see, in English, the simple present tense verb is formed by *to be* verb followed by the main verb, as in:

I am eating.

To express this tense in Persian, we do not need to put the equivalent for the auxiliary verb *am*. That is, we just add *mi-* at the front of the main verb, as in:

man   mi-xor-am
I   eat-I
I am eating.

Thus, it wrong to say: *hast-am mi-xor-am* for *I am eating.*

The same is right for other auxiliary verbs in English. For example to question a sentence, we use *do* or *did*, as in:

Why did you hit him?

In Persian, we do not need to put the equivalent for did and we say the sentence just in past tense, as in:

čerä   šomä un   rä   zad-in
why   you him OM   hit-you
'Why did you hit him?'

but we can not say:

čerä   šomä kard-in un   rä   zad-in

Second verb:

In Persian, when there are two verbs in a sentence, the first verb comes in the present tense form, that is, with *mi-* and the second verb takes the prefix *be-,* as in:

man   mi-xäh-am   qazä   be-xor-am

I   want-I   food   eat-I

I want to eat food.

When there are two verbs and two objects in the sentence, the word order is: first verb, first object, second object and second verb, as in:

man   mi-xäh-am be sag-am   qazä   be-dah-am

I   want-I   to dog-my   food   give-I

I want to give food to my dog.

Pronoun:

Pronoun is a word, which is used instead of a name that is already mentioned. For example in *John went home*, we can replace *John* by *he* as in:

He went home.

He is a pronoun in English. This type of pronoun is called personal pronoun and can replace the subject. Other personal pronouns are *I, you, she, it, we, they.*

There are similar pronouns in Persian, which can replace the subject. The English pronouns and their Persian equivalents are :

I	man	we	mä
you	to	you (pl)	šomä
he/she/it	un	they	unhä

Sentence types:

Like any other language, there are different sentence types in Persian. The main word order in the sentence is Subject + Object + Verb (SOV). The other sentence types are as in below:

1. Sentence without an object:

man mi-dav-am
S   V
I   run-I
I am running.

2. Sentence with a direct object:

man	sib rä	mi-xor-am
S	DO	V
I	apple-OM	eat-I

I am eating the apple.

3. Sentence with an indirect object:

man	be madrese	mi-rav-am
S	IO	V
I	to school	go-I

I am going to school.

4. Sentence with both direct and indirect objects:

man	sib rä	be Ali	mi-dah-am
S	DO	IO	V
I	apple OM	to Ali	give-I

I am giving the apple to Ali.

5. Sentence with two indirect objects:

man	az xäne	be madrese	mi-rav-am
S	IO1	IO2	V
I	from home	to school	go-I

I am going from home to school.

Subject:

Subject is a noun or pronoun which does the action of the verb and usually comes at the beginning of the sentence, as in
John went home yesterday, *John* is the subject of the sentence who has done the action of going.

In Persian, subject can be deleted from the sentence, because there is a personal suffix at the end of the verb which specifies the subject, as in:

man be xäne raftam
I   to   home   went-I
I went home.

man 'I' is the subject and can be deleted because the suffix *-am* at the end of the verb shows that the subject is the first person singular even it is deleted:
be xäne raftam

Suffixes:

There are different suffixes in Persian which come at the end of the verb and show whether the verb is in a specific tense or mode. The important suffixes in Persian are verb endings as follow:

I am	-am
You are	-i
He/She/It is	-e (ast)[85]
We are	-im
You are	-in
They are	-and
I was	-bud am
You were	-bud i
He/She/It was	-bud[86]
We were	-bud im
You were	-bud in
They were	-bud and
Noun suffixes	
My hand	dast am
My	-am
Your	-et
His/her/its	-eš
Our	-emun
Your	-etun
Their	-ešun

tä:

The word '*tä*' has different usages:

1. showing duration:

    az sä'at-e dah-e sobh **tä** daväzdah

---

[85] This suffix for other verbs is –*ad*.
[86] The suffix for other verbs is *and*.

from ten to twelve o'clock

2. showing distance:

az xäne **tä** madrese

from home to school

3. acting as a classifier after a number and before a noun:

dah **tä** ketäb

ten books

Suffix –i (able):
The suffix –*i* can be added to the infinitive forms of verbs to mean *able*. For example:
xordan (eating) + *i* = xordani (edible)
didan (seein) + *i* = didani (see-able)
xändan (reading) + *i* = xändani (read-able)

Tag questions:
The tag question word in Persian is 'mage na' that unlike English can be used with any tense and any verb, as in:
havä emruz xeyli sard hast, mage na
weather today very cold is, but not
The weather is very cold today, is not it?

to diruz   be madrese raft-i, mage na
you yesterday to school   went-you, but not
You went to school yesterday, did not you?

tavän, xäh and dän:

The verbs *tavän* 'can', *xäh* 'want' and *'dän'* know' have no simple past form and the past continues form is used for both tenses:

man midänestm ke un miravad
I   knew-I   that he go-he
I knew that he was going.

If the verb *xah* is used in the past tense form, the meaning is negative:

man xäštam beravam vali dir bud.
I   wanted-I go-I   but late was
I wanted to go but it was late.

There and it:

In English, some sentences start with '*it*' or '*there*'. These two words have no meaning and just fill in the subject position. That is why they are called empty or expletive pronouns. See these examples:

It is raining.

There is a book on the table.

In Persian, we do not need an equivalent for these words:

bärän mi-bär-ad

rain   rain-is

It is raining.

but we can not say: un mi-bär-ad

For *there*, we can say:

yek ketäb ruye   miz hast

one book on   table is

There is a book on the table.

But we can not say: unjä yek ketäb ruye miz hast.

Transitive verbs:

A sentence can be without an object. The verb in this type of sentence is called intransitive verb, as in these sentences:

man raftam   I went

to ämadi   you came

un xäbid   he/she slept

If a sentence have one direct object, the verb in this sentence is called a transitive verb:

man äb xord-am

I water drank-I

I drank water.

to ketäb xänd-i

you book read-you

you read a book.

un Ali rä did

she Ali OM saw

She saw Ali.

A sentence can have just one indirect object.

man be xäne miravam	I am going home.
to az bäq umadi	You came from the garden.
un bä dočarxe raft	He weny by bike.

A sentence can have one direct object and one indirect object.

<u>man</u>	<u>äb rä</u>	<u>be gorbe</u>	<u>dädam</u>
S	DO	IO	V

I gave the water to the cat.

Verb:

Verb is a word, which specifies the action or state of the subject. For example, in *John went home*, the verb *went* specifies the action of *going*, which has taken place by *John*. In English, verbs do not have an ending for different persons. The only change is for the third person singular (i.e. *it, she, and he*), which takes *(e)s* in the present tense, as in:

I go

You go

He goes

We go

You go

They go

However, in Persian, verbs change for different persons. That is, for every person, there is a different suffix at the end of the verb. This suffix shows whether the subject is *I, you, he, she*, etc. For example, the verb *rav* (go) will be like this for different persons:

mi-rav-am	I go
mi-rav-i	You go
mi-rav-ad	He goes
mi-rav-im	We go
mi-rav-id	You go
mi-rav-and	They go

Therefore, there are different personal suffixes at the end of the verb. These suffixes are:

I	am	we	im
you	i	you (pl)	id
he/she/it	ad	they	and

Verbs plus prepositions:

Most verbs in Persian need a preposition which comes before the object in the same sentence. It is always challenging for the Persian students to use them. Some examples are:

tašakor kardan az	thanking from	to thank
telefon kardan be	telephoning to	to call
porsidan az	asking from	to ask
piše man biya	come to near me	come to me

Vowel y:

When there is one vowel after another one, usually *y* is inserted between them. For example, in *mi-äy-am* 'I am coming'
As you see, a *y* is inserted and it becomes *miyäyam*.

Vowel e:

This vowel has three different usages:

1- Possessive *e: ketäb e Ali*
2- Short version of '*hast*':

bist   säl e   ke dars   mixän-am
twenty year is that lesson read-I
It is twenty years that I am studying.

3- Marker for past participle form of verbs: *rafte-am*, I have gone.

When the vowel e is not written, at the end of word it is written as (ο) and is a part of a word:
un bist sal-e hast.
he twenty year is
He is twenty years old.

Word če:
When there is the question word *če* (what) before a noun, we add the suffix *i* to the noun, as in:
Šomä   če ruz-i   ämadin
you   what day   came
What day did you come?

Conclusion

This book has been designed as a comprehensive and practical guide for anyone who wishes to learn Persian (Farsi and Dari) as a second or foreign language. Its distinctive approach—based on comparative linguistics—empowers learners to understand Persian through the lens of English, making the process logical and efficient. By focusing on structural differences and similarities, the book helps learners avoid common pitfalls and accelerates their ability to communicate confidently.

The inclusion of transliteration removes one of the greatest barriers for beginners: the need to master a non-Roman script before speaking the language. This feature allows learners to concentrate on pronunciation, vocabulary, and sentence structure without being overwhelmed by orthography. At the same time, the book introduces the Persian alphabet for those who wish to progress further.

Covering both Farsi and Dari variations, this resource ensures learners can communicate effectively across Iran and Afghanistan. The lessons are practical, culturally informed, and supported by a detailed grammar section that addresses subtleties often overlooked in other textbooks. From everyday conversations to essential grammar rules, this book equips learners with the tools they need to speak Persian naturally and accurately.

Ultimately, learning a language is not just about memorizing words—it is about understanding how those words work together to create meaning. This book provides that understanding. With consistent practice and the guidance offered here, learners will find Persian not only accessible but enjoyable. May this book serve as a bridge to new opportunities, cultural appreciation, and meaningful communication.

About the Author

Yavar Dehghani is an experienced linguist and educator specializing in Persian language instruction for English speakers. With years of teaching experience in Australia, Yavar has developed a unique comparative linguistics approach that simplifies the process of learning Persian by highlighting structural differences and similarities between English and Persian. This method has proven highly effective for adult learners, enabling them to achieve fluency faster and with greater confidence.

Yavar's passion for language learning extends beyond the classroom. As the author of bilingual dictionaries and language resources, Yavar is committed to making Persian accessible to learners worldwide. By combining practical lessons, cultural insights, and clear grammatical explanations, Yavar's work bridges the gap between theory and real-world communication.

www.yadehghani.com

www.ingramcontent.com/pod-product-compliance
Lightning Source LLC
Chambersburg PA
CBHW051836090426
42736CB00011B/1825